VINT

AMADER SHA

Gaura Pant 'Shivani' (1923–2003) was among the foremost Hindi
writers of her time. Born in Rajkot, her childhood was spent in
various places as her father moved from one princely state to another.
As a young child, she was tutored by her scholar grandfather, Pandit
Hariram Pande, a close associate of Pandit Madan Mohan Malviya
and one of the founding faculty members of Banaras Hindu University.
At the age of twelve, she was sent, along with her two siblings, to
Shantiniketan, where she spent nine magical years. Throughout her
life, Shivani lived by the teachings of her gurus at the Ashram and
looked upon Bengal as her second home. Her literary output that
spans some forty works bears the deep imprint of both Kumaon
and Bengal. Best known for her short stories, novels and newspaper
columns, Shivani also wrote several travelogues and a three-part
autobiography. She was awarded the Padma Shri in 1982.

Ira Pande started her career as a lecturer in Panjab University, and later
worked with several prominent English language publishing houses.
Her last editorial stint was as chief editor of the India International
Centre's Publication Division. In 2005, she wrote a memoir of her
mother titled *Diddi: My Mother's Voice*, documenting the life and
times of Shivani. In 2010, she got the Sahitya Akademi Award for
her translation of Manohar Shyam Joshi's *T'ta Professor*, which also
won the Crossword Book Award for translation. She writes a regular
column for the *Tribune*.

BY THE SAME TRANSLATOR

AMADER SHANTINIKETAN

Shivani

TRANSLATED BY
Ira Pande

VINTAGE
An imprint of Penguin Random House

VINTAGE

USA | Canada | UK | Ireland | Australia
New Zealand | India | South Africa | China

Vintage is part of the Penguin Random House group of companies
whose addresses can be found at global.penguinrandomhouse.com

Published by Penguin Random House India Pvt. Ltd.
4th Floor, Capital Tower 1, MG Road,
Gurugram 122 002, Haryana, India

Penguin
Random House
India

First published in Vintage by Penguin Random House India 2021

ISBN 9780143458678

Typeset in Berkeley by Manipal Technologies Limited, Manipal
Printed at Replika Press Pvt. Ltd, India

www.penguin.co.in

Contents

Contents

Introduction

Amader Shantiniketan was written by our mother, Shivani, sometime in the early 1960s and published by New Age Publishers, Calcutta. Although I do not remember that time very clearly, I am pretty sure that it was neither circulated widely nor promoted, since in those days books were never pushed as aggressively as they are now. The publishers also never thought it necessary to give Shivani a royalty, information about any subsequent editions or details of sales. Shivani was a strangely trusting soul and once she handed over a book to a publisher, she seldom inquired about how it was doing or whether it had been reviewed. So that was that.

Mercifully, the publishers shut shop one day and, quite in keeping with their quaint work ethic, did not think it fit to inform Shivani of what would happen to her book. There was another twist in this tale: my mother always wrote by hand and submitted a handwritten manuscript to her publishers without bothering to keep a copy. I have no idea how she managed to get another publisher to bring out a fresh edition. Perhaps she dug out a personal copy to give them a master file. Whatever the truth, this charming memoir is among the books we inherited after her death when her estate was transferred to us four siblings according to her will.

My sister Mrinal worked meticulously on every book, editing each one beautifully and working closely with the new publishers to ensure that the books were elegantly brought out. It is largely thanks to her efforts that there is a handsome set of Shivani's complete works in the market today. Our effort now is to get as many of them translated into English as we can so that a new generation of readers—many of whom do not read Hindi any more—can access her work. A few years ago, I translated some of her short stories and essays into English to form the core of my memoir of her life, *Diddi: My Mother's Voice*. It was so warmly received that I did another one a few years later, titled *Apradhini: Women without Men*, on a remarkable collection of stories and essays she had written on jailed women. I fear that our general attitude to translated works is so dismissive that it did not reach out to the readers I would have liked to interest. Perhaps, one day, its karma will ensure it gets the attention it so richly deserves.

This charming memoir was written by Shivani almost fifty years ago and it documents her stay in Shantiniketan from 1935 to 1944. It has always been one of my favourite reads, and for a long time I had meant to translate it into English one day. Someone had already done a Marathi version during her lifetime but I had not been able to read it since I do not know Marathi. When I got down to it, I realized that it was too slim to make a stand-alone book, so I decided to add some of the magnificent tributes she wrote when any of her dear contemporaries passed away.

This section forms the second half of the book and is a sort of diptych to the time she remembers so warmly in the first half. I think it works well.

There is another reason why I think this is an appropriate time for this book to be published. For one, the state of education—particularly primary education—has hit such a nadir that it is imperative we breathe fresh life into it. There are some excellent new schools that are trying hard to make learning an adventure and a life-altering experience, but they remain confined to small pockets and are in many cases so expensive that only a privileged few can hope to benefit from their efforts. We venerate Tagore for many things: his poetry, his music, his writings and his thoughts on nationalism. But to me, his greatest contribution was to introduce a pedagogy that was inspired by the ancient system of the ashram and *gurukul*. Moreover, by creating in a remote corner of Bengal a cosmopolitan culture where students came not just from the four corners of India but from China, Japan, Ceylon and even Java and Sumatra, he opened minds and hearts in a way that is so vital for embedding messages of harmony and love in young minds.

As you read this book you will realize just how this experiment in international living ignited new energies and a cultural cross-pollination that was so much a part of our ancient Buddhist and Indian traditions. Living in the warmth of a family of gurus was a liberating experience that few were untouched by. Throughout her life, Shivani remained an extraordinary teacher, and if her children have achieved anything in their lives, it is in no small measure due to the element of joy she brought to learning. It was a legacy of her own time in the Ashram and a quality I saw in each of her friends from there. Sadly, not one of them is alive today to read this book, but I remember a story she told us (one of many, I may add) that really amused her. She would call Amartya Sen 'Babloo' when she referred to him—even though she never met him after she left Shantiniketan—having known his mother (Amita di to her), who visited her father and Shivani's guru, Acharya Kshiti Mohan Sen, during the summer break. 'I remember him sitting in my lap as a tiny tot, and look at him today!' she would chuckle.

There is not much that I can add to the text of this memoir but I do wish to acknowledge the help and support I have received from my siblings: Veena Joshi, Mrinal Pande and Muktesh Pant. I would also like to thank my friend Radharani Mitra for help with the Bengali parts of the text. I wish to dedicate this version of *Amader Shantiniketan* to all of Shivani's grandchildren and great-grandchildren in the hope that they will all carry some part of her in their lives and keep the memory of an extraordinary soul alive almost a century after her birth.

Ira Pande
Noida, 2020

PART I

Amader Shantiniketan

Amader Shantiniketan

As I sit down to remember all those teachers who have inspired me, a kaleidoscope flashes past my eyes. Like a Buddhist prayer wheel that mesmerizes one with its ceaseless turns, the images suck me into a tunnel that takes me very far back. I tumble down that abyss and see several faces rescued from the mists of time. Some of them are serious and sombre, others smile or laugh. At the end of this magical tunnel, it seems to me as if almost the entire faculty of Shantiniketan—like a line-up of debt collectors—waits for me to pay back what I owe them.

Let me start at the very beginning: from the day I first met Gurudev in 1935.

My older sister, Jayanti, our brother, Tribhuvan, and I had come to Shantiniketan all the way from Almora. As the youngest of the three siblings, I was admitted to Path Bhavan, the school section of the Ashram. Soon after we settled in, the Path Bhavan principal, Dr Dhirendra Mohan Sen, took Jayanti and me to meet Gurudev. We reached Gurudev's home,

'Uttarayan', and were told that he was writing in another part of the house, known as 'Shyamali'.

The evening shadows were falling and the blood-red earth turned dark as we neared Gurudev's chair. Dressed in a long black gown, the black cap he wore on his head highlighted his broad forehead and glowing face, and his eyes seemed lit up with an inner light. No wonder the Ashramites considered him the Guru of gurus. And yet, this towering figure was also among the gentlest and kindest of men. His serene and compassionate gaze included everyone in a warm embrace—rich or poor, big or small.

All of us, whether we came from India or Japan, China or Sri Lanka or wherever, stood before him every morning as children who had come to an enchanted garden. At the morning prayer assembly held every day in front of the Ashram library, we met the Buddhist scholar Fan-chu, who had come all the way from China, as well as Khairuddin, a Muslim student from Sumatra, Susheela from Gujarat, and Kumudini from—what then seemed to us a foreign land—Kerala. All of us stood, with folded hands and closed eyes, as we sang the hymns he had composed. Never once do I remember anyone trying to jostle someone or giggle or push. Such was the respect Gurudev evoked in all of us that whenever we were in his presence, we became better human beings.

He looked up as we came near, and never, for as long as I live, will I forget that moment. Framed against the glow of the setting sun, he looked unlike any human being I had ever seen, and to my child's eyes, he seemed to be what I imagined God would look like. Of their own volition, our hands came together and Jayanti and I bowed at his feet. His hand passed lovingly over our heads and he smiled as he asked gently, 'Are you very homesick?' How did he know, I wondered.

'Learn to speak Bangla then,' his soft voice urged us, 'and you will never be homesick. Wait, I'll introduce you to Pupe.'

'Banmali,' he called out and his favourite companion ran out. 'Go and call Didi, will you?' We were then introduced to both his granddaughters and invited to share a meal with them that evening. Gurudev's daughter-in-law, Pratima di, otherwise known as 'Bouthan' in the Ashram, presided over the table.

'These two girls have come from very far. They can't speak Bengali and look a little scared to me,' he said to her. 'After dinner will you take them to the rehearsal? That might cheer them up.'

So after dinner, his granddaughter Nandita (whose nickname was Burhi), took us on a guided tour of Uttarayan before she led us to the room where the rehearsal for a new dance drama, *Varshamangal*, was taking place.

A large, airy space framed with open windows on all sides, the rehearsal room was placed like a jewel in the centre of Gurudev's garden. In one corner was a collection of brightly polished copper and brass pots from Kumaon, while a huge wooden divan from Jamnagar was set against a wall. Gurudev himself sat on this, leaning against the bright Santhali and Burmese cushions as he directed the performers. Near him, on the floor, sat the musicians—Shailajaranjan Majumdar, Shantimoy Ghosh, Shishir da, Santosh da—as well as the students taking part in the drama.

My eyes had scarcely taken all this in when, with a dramatic burst of bells, a tall dancer, Nivedita di, glided across

the polished floor. Our jaws hung open with wonder and we
forgot all our homesickness as the dancer and the song, with
its mesmeric rhythm, cast a spell:

> *Hridoy amar naache re aajike*
> *Mayurero moto naache re . . .*

> [My heart dances today
> Like a peacock it dances . . .]

Our heads swung entranced from the dancer to the singers:
the deep bass of Shanti da mingled with the sweet soprano
voices of Kanika and Amita di; all of them blended with a
melody on the sitar so beautifully that I felt even the stars
outside were dancing. Everyone seemed totally immersed in
the mood of that dance, especially the sitar player who was
bent in ecstasy, his eyes closed in rapture as he played along.
His long fingers slid over the strings of the sitar and cast a
spell that was difficult to break.

Gradually, over the next few months, I learnt Bangla,
and the joy that I derived from this knowledge has stayed
with me to this day. I am proud to tell you that it was
Gurudev himself who taught me the alphabet, lovingly
guiding me through the basic primer, *Sahaj Path*. Of course
there were some hilarious moments. '*Bone thake bagh, gachhe
thake pakhi* [The tiger lives in the forest, the bird in the
tree]' was one of the opening lessons. In my excitement at
having mastered this difficult line, I read it out to Gurudev
as: '*Gachhe thake bagh, bone thake pakhi* [The tiger lives on
the tree, the bird in the forest].'

Gurudev sat patiently, waiting for me to finish, but the famous Bengali novelist Charubabu, who was sitting by his side, shook with silent mirth, his vast body rippling as he tried to contain his laughter. Oblivious to my mistake, I went through the entire lesson and turned eagerly to Gurudev for praise. He looked gravely at me and asked: 'So, child! Do tigers live in trees in your part of the world?'

I remember another delightful instance. Until a brilliant Tamil student, Shivshankar Mundukur, joined the Ashram, I was the star of my class. I was Dr Alex Aronson's favourite student and basked in this fact. However, under the brilliance of this new entrant, my reputation stood threatened. One day, Dr Aronson asked us to write a critical appraisal of a Keats poem and bring it the next day. I ran straight to Gurudev. 'Please write it for me,' I begged him. 'I don't want that Tamil boy to do better. Please, please, please, Gurudev.'

He almost threw me out but when I refused to budge, he dictated a brilliant piece that more than matched the Keats poem. The next day, I confidently submitted my assignment, secure in the knowledge that a Nobel laureate in literature had written it. So imagine my horror when we got our papers back—that wretched Tamilian genius had been awarded a 6 while I had a measly 4 out of 10! Even more insulting was what Dr Aronson had scrawled at the end of my paper: 'Too elusive.' I ran straight to Gurudev. 'You always tell us to honour our foreign teachers and look what they do! He's given you just 4 out of 10!' Gurudev threw back his head as he laughed. 'Don't tell anyone I wrote it,' he told me in confidence.

The other incident was a childish attempt at poetry writing. Every month, a literary soiree was organized. Sometimes it was for the little ones in Shishu Bhavan, sometimes for the middle-school scholars of Path Bhavan and sometimes for the college students of Shiksha Bhavan. Gurudev would give us the first line of a poem and each contestant got five minutes in which to compose the next. I normally didn't dare enter the contest because the others were all outstanding students, among them my own brother Tribhuvan, who was a formidable rival. He was among Gurudev's favourite students and had become a handsome, confident young man by then. Above all, he was so quick-witted that he had virtually no rival in the department of repartee. Anyway, I put up my hand for the contest. That day, Gurudev had chosen the first line as 'If I were a boy' for the girls and 'If I were a girl' for the boys to complete.

I brought the house down with my entry: 'If I were a boy, what would become of the boy I love?' I thumbed my nose at my brother as I proudly went to receive my prize from Gurudev. For the rest of the week, however, I had to put up with cheeky remarks like, 'So who's the lucky one, eh?'

~

My sister Jayanti and I soon became fluent in Bangla but the same could not be said of Tribhuvan. So, whereas both Jayanti and I spoke flawless Bangla (polished to perfection by Ramesh da, who was nicknamed Pandit Moshai because of the long pigtail he sported), Tribhi refused to pollute his tongue with it, preferring snootily to speak in English instead. One day, when the three of us were standing together, Gurudev turned to Tribhi and said sternly, 'Your sisters speak Bangla like natives yet you refuse to let go of English, don't you? From today, I want you to speak only in Bangla, do you understand?'

How could poor Tribhi dare to speak any other language after this? He first tried out his halting Bangla in the students' mess one evening. The Ashram cook, Harihar Prabhakar, was especially partial to us non-Bengali students and often slyly slipped us an extra treat (like an egg or a fish-head) as he asked, 'Aha! What faraway land do you come from, Didi?' That evening, Prabhakar had cooked fish for dinner. In his eagerness to show off his new mastery of Bangla, my brother's deep baritone rang out clearly over the din: 'Harihar Prabhakar! *Aaj aamake maach khabe!* [Today, the fish will eat me!]'. Poor Tribhi, he had actually wanted to say that he would eat fish that day but his tongue was hopelessly mixed up.

A roar of derisive laughter rose from the tables. The next day, no doubt after someone had related this incident to Gurudev, Tribhi was asked to come up to him after a lecture.

In front of all the students of Shiksha Bhavan, Gurudev told Tribhi, '*Thaak Tribhuvan! Toke aar Bangla shikhte hoube na aar maachh-o toke khabe na!* [Stop right there, Tribhuvan! From now on, you need neither speak Bangla, nor will a fish eat you!]'

~

Each year, Uttarayan held a literary festival and a host of eminent writers assembled to take part in it. For us, this was an event to cherish and we'd run from one great writer to another to seek their autographs. I still have those of Jaladhar Sen, Charubabu, Narendra Mishra and Sajanikanta Das, among others. At one of these festivals, Gurudev asked me to recite one of his famous poems:

> Sanyasi Upagupta
> Mathurapurir prachirer tole
> Ekoda chhilen supto . . .

When he introduced me, he mentioned how happy he was that despite being a Kumaoni student, my Bangla pronunciation was flawless. As a bonus, my autograph book was soon full of famous names; some of them had accompanying verses as well. It was the subject of envy among my fellow students for years. Many poems were specially written for me by name. One of these was:

> Himalayer kanya toomi Gaurir moton
> Jibone phutiyo haansi phulera jemon
> Shooale re bhalo beshe koro aapnaar
> Shantir nirjhor
> Jibone tomar
>
> [You are like the daughter of the Himalayas, Gauri
> May you always smile like a flower!
> Make everyone yours through love
> And may God continue to shower peace upon
> you all your life]

I could have exchanged that autograph book for anything; one friend even offered me his entire stamp collection for Jaladhar Sen's autograph. Jaladhar Sen had become very frail by then and it was not easy to persuade him to write, so how could I even think of such an exchange? Gurudev himself drew a sketch of me and a Japanese student, Mayaki, on the first page of that precious autograph book! I guard it with my life even now.

~

While on the subject, it is time to confess to an incident that I regret even now. Often, in the summers, Gurudev would come to Almora. Naturally, we spent all our time there and his daughter-in-law, Pratima di—whom we all called Bouthan—was his constant companion. Along with her came his granddaughter, Nandita, who was my friend. Pratima di treated me exactly as she did her own daughter, cooking us special treats, telling us bedtime stories, soothing fevered brows and even plaiting my hair whenever I went across. At every Durga Puja, we both were gifted identical saris.

Once, when Gurudev was busy writing as usual, she emerged from the house to ask him what to do with a beautiful silk gown he had been gifted in China. 'The moths have attacked it and made so many holes, it can't be repaired,' she told him. 'What shall I do with it?'

Without lifting his eyes from his desk, Gurudev said, 'Give it to these girls, they can make blouses from it.'

Both Nandita and I scooped up the discarded robe and ran to make it into two identical blouses. Neither of us realized what sacrilege we were performing. How I wish I had preserved that robe as a blessed garment.

In the summer of 1937, I accompanied Gurudev's party to Almora. Along with him were his secretary, Annada, and his granddaughter Nandita. Scores of his admirers would line up outside his compartment whenever the train stopped and offer garlands. As soon as the train moved on, he would hand over the garlands to me. I am reminded of a verse he himself had written:

> Nana loke nana peyechhe ratan
> Ami aniyachi koriya jatan
> Tomar kanthe de bar moton
> Rajkanther mala . . .
>
> [Others got jewels
> but I offer you a flower garland
> that hung from the royal neck]

Even now, after all these years, I feel so proud that I once held the garlands he handed over to me.

~

I also recall a hilarious incident from those days. For some unknown reason, the Ashram kitchen had decided to bury us poor Ashramites under a deluge of aloo-parwal—potatoes cooked with a gourd known in Bengal as potol. It seemed as if the person in charge of the students' mess had bought mountains of the vegetables at knock-down prices and we were doomed to eat them for the rest of the year. So for breakfast we were fed potol bhaja (fried parwal), lunch was potoler dolma (stuffed parwal), while dinner was often a watery potol jhol or curry. They even dared to add the wretched potol to the delicious hilsa fish that was occasionally cooked as a special treat. For some time, we bore this unexpected avalanche with fortitude but after a while, rumbles of protest started to emerge. Among the students were some members of the royal houses of Tripura and Cooch Behar, an odd prince from Burma and foreign students from Lanka and Java. Their misery soon became palpable. Initially, we went on a silent protest. Then, when there was no response, another form of protest was launched. The dining hall had a large blackboard at its entrance that was used to post messages and notices. One night, a brave person wiped it clean of all its notices and drew a huge cartoon of a potato and a potol. To make the message clear to all, the phantom cartoonist had chopped the 'heads' of the offending vegetables and written neatly under each: 'Dhik aloo! [Fie potato!]' and 'Dhik potol! [Fie parwal!]'.

Still, nothing happened, and potato and potol continued to arrive with disgusting regularity on our plates.

So we all marched as a delegation to Suren da, who looked after the affairs of the common mess. We urged him to do something but, being a man of few words, he listened politely and smiled quietly to himself. 'You are students of an Ashram,' he reminded us gently. 'You will have to learn to like simple food and adopt austerity. After all, simple living and high thinking are what you were sent here to learn, isn't it?'

'But, Suren da,' one of the delegates protested, 'simple living does not mean that we eat the same vegetables every day!'

Suren da ignored this and indicated that he would add nothing to what he had said earlier. We returned disappointed, but decided to fight on for our right to decent meals. Another day went by and it was decided that we would now go to Gurudev himself and tell him our sad tale.

By this time, Gurudev had moved to 'Punashcha' as his earlier retreat, Shyamali, had been torn down. As usual, he was busy writing when we reached. At his feet sat his favourite acolyte, Aloo da. Aloo da had been named after his round, bald pate that resembled a large potato. In fact, the tiny, sparkling eyes embedded in that fleshy face were not unlike the eyes of a potato. All in all, name and face were a perfect match, we felt. Those days, he functioned as Gurudev's personal secretary and followed his Guru like a shadow. He was also an important part of every dance drama composed by Gurudev and his opinion was respected by all the performers. Moreover, he was a natural clown and his store of jokes and funny stories was limitless; he had something amusing to say at every gathering. And when his audience rocked with laughter, Aloo da stood quietly, with a deadpan expression. He was a riot! Those who saw him in *Tasher Desh* will know what I am trying to say. His acting skills were unforgettable.

Aloo da's eyes began to glint wickedly as soon as he spotted us, for he realized that we must have come with some tale of woe. Gurudev greeted us with his usual warmth and made us sit down. Then he called out to Banmali to bring out the glass jar he kept for such occasions. Each one of us was handed a toffee, and then he asked, 'So? What brings you all here today? Do I have to be the chief guest at another one of your literary evenings, or has a needle pricked your washerwoman's finger again?'

He was referring to an incident that had taken place a few days ago. Some student had carelessly left a needle in a garment he had given for washing and the poor washerwoman's finger had turned septic after she pricked it while washing. We all ran around gathering donations for her treatment at a hospital in Calcutta. The most generous donor had been Gurudev himself. When no one else seemed to be able to answer him, I got up and bravely started: 'Please, Gurudev, deliver us from aloo-potol!'

When the others nodded vigorously, I went on: 'For the last month, all we've been fed are unending dishes of these two vegetables. As if it wasn't enough for the cooks to feed us aloo at every meal, they have doubled that torture by adding potol as well. For the last month, all we've seen is aloo and potol, nothing else!'

We all waited for his reaction to this outburst. But before he could open his mouth, Aloo da quietly got up and, gathering his dhoti around him, touched Gurudev's feet as he started to leave.

'What happened?' Gurudev asked, puzzled at this sudden departure. 'Where are you off to?'

Two large teardrops fell from Aloo da's eyes as he answered in strangled tones: 'Can't you see, Maharaj? How can I stay here after what these children have just told you? I am going to collect Potol and then I'll bid the Ashram goodbye!'

Our protest dissipated into laughter. We ran to Aloo da and dragged him back to sit with us. Potol da was Aloo da's younger brother, who had suffered a serious brain injury many years ago and had come to Gurudev's Ashram with his brother. You could see him on certain nights, lantern in hand, going round and round the Ashram, his strange voice making stranger noises as he kept guard. How could we have been so unthinking when we launched our tirade against aloo and potol!

That evening, however, we were delighted to find that even if we fished deeply into our curries, there was not a trace of potato or potol to be found!

Many scholars and writers have written about Tagore's musical compositions, his literature, philosophy and painting. Doubtless, that is the Tagore the world deserves to know about. But to us children, he was a guru, a loving father figure above all. Poetry, plays, novels, painting, music, dance direction—if Tagore cared deeply for something beyond all of these, it was us Ashramites. It is hard to believe that this towering world figure could take the time to settle the humble matter of potato and potol overkill for his students.

~

Visva Bharati was Gurudev's ultimate sanctuary and retreat: a place where a prince sat on the same wooden bench as an ordinary student at mealtimes and under the canopy of the same tree while learning a lesson.

As a child, when Tagore's parents sent him to Bengal Academy, he felt he had been dispatched to a jail. He has written somewhere about this: 'We hardly ever understood completely what our teachers taught us. We were never inspired to make the effort to try and understand it nor were the school authorities especially bothered about this. Now I have a sanctuary of my own. The children who come here are mischievous but what else can they be if they are children? As for the teachers here, they may occasionally lose patience with these naughty children but whenever they consider punishment I try and remind them of their own childhood and the matter gets sorted out without a problem.'

This is the reason why no student was ever punished in the Ashram. In the eight years that I spent there, just two students were sent away. There was no corporal punishment by order of Gurudev himself, although occasionally, the teachers did transgress this rule. However, this happened only under the rarest circumstances and generally with the consent of the student himself! I do remember our being asked to stand in a corner as a punishment, though. When this happened, the student stood with a long face under a tree away from the rest of his classmates, and became the butt of ribbing and unkind comments from the neighbouring classes sitting under the nearby trees. How we dreaded those missiles! Once in a while, the cook Prabhakar or one of his assistants would spot us and turn his head away to muffle his giggle, or wag a finger in the direction of the punished soul. Later, when we were in the dining hall, he would come close and ask in a loud whisper, 'So, Didimoni, why were you punished today?', and the titters would start again.

Tagore tried to rectify all the wrongs that appeared to him as blights from his own schooldays. So in Shantiniketan, every student was free to study (or not study) any subject. If you were learning music at Sangeet Bhavan, you could stroll into any class in Shiksha Bhavan (the college section) if you wanted. The tender hearts of children were never burdened with heavy courses. Our textbooks were

imaginatively compiled, full of colourful illustrations and
covered in soft covers that were easy to handle and keep.
In fact, they looked like brightly coloured boxes of sweets.
For the nursery children, there was a special class called
'Golper Class' meant only for stories and tales. Whenever
we heard that Tagore himself or his talented artist nephew,
Abanindranath Tagore, was going to take it, we ran to attend
it, never mind that we were by then in college! I can tell
you that before the magic of the Tagore tales, even Hans
Christian Andersen and the Brothers Grimm paled. I can
remember one particular story even after all these years,
called 'Momer Putul [The Wax Doll]'. We sat through three
periods to hear its end and missed all our regular classes.
Such was the magic of the Tagore imagination!

Our classes were held in the sprawling field outside
Sinha Sadan, under a cluster of shady trees. On any day, you
could walk into a Hindi class conducted by Acharya Hajari
Prasad Dwivedi. Or, if you wished, you could stroll over to
any one of the neighbouring 'classes' where you could either
listen to the German professor Dr Alex Aronson's lecture
on Shakespeare's plays or hear Marjorie Sykes's lectures on
English literature, or to Professor Adhikari as he conducted
classes on Hindu philosophy and yoga. Floating above them
all were the haunting strains of Shailaj da playing a new
melody composed for his *israj* by Gurudev himself. We
were the first to sing with full-throated enthusiasm Tagore's
famous hymn to Bengal, '*Amaar shonar Bangla, aami tomaay
bhalo bashi* . . . [I love you, my golden land of Bengal . . .]'.
Although we were not to know then that one day it would
be adopted as the national anthem of Bangladesh, from the

moment we heard its stirring lyrics, we realized this was a song that had the power to change destinies. Perhaps this is why Shanti da (Shantimoy Ghosh) got up and danced like a man possessed that day, and each one of us, no matter how unmusical, felt our feet tap-tapping on their own to its compulsive beat. During the Second World War, when the battles on the eastern front of India had led to a few Japanese bombs being dropped on Calcutta, a slight shiver of apprehension reached our peaceful Ashram as well. Gurudev's reaction to this was a beautiful composition, 'Hingshay unmotto prithvi . . . [A world crazed by violence . . .]', and it was as if a gentle breeze had magically blown away the war clouds from our horizon.

Shantiniketan was the kind of peaceful retreat that remained unshaken by the din and terror of the world beyond. Tagore managed to imbue it with a spirit that banished all evil and negative energy from its precincts. Perhaps this was why it resolutely refused to stifle the spirit of its students. Our classes were not closed in within walls that shut out the outer world, nor did they have ceilings to close our minds. As we sat under the canopy of the Ashram's trees, the blue sky spread over us for as far as we could see. Never did any teacher ever admonish a student for following the flight of a bird. If our fingers ached after writing, we were free to put down our pens and stroll away to hear the Santhal tribals who often passed the Ashram's fields as they went about their work, singing or playing a haunting melody on a flute. When we tired of doing geometry or algebra, we were not punished for letting our minds wander or for following the dance of squirrels as they chased each other up a tree. The cooing doves and pigeons came to entertain us and helped us learn the dates of the three battles of Panipat so painlessly that they have remained etched in our minds forever. Like scores of students before and after us, we also struggled with Akbar's religious policy and Lord Bentinck's administrative reforms, yet what else was it for but the magic of the Ashram that these never became a tiresome burden? Interestingly, for all the freedom we had, the Ashram bred in each one of us a sense of self-control. Our freedom actually disciplined our minds.

~

All the students of the Ashram had to leave their beds before sunrise. Three bells marked the time for this and the punishment for the lazybones who could not rouse themselves was: no breakfast. Then, we made our beds, had a bath and lined up outside the library for our morning assembly. Each morning and evening, the start of the school day and its end was marked by a prayer. Tagore himself composed these hymns and set them to beautiful ragas such as Bhairavi, Vibhas or Bhairav. The unforgettable music of 'Bhengechho duaar, eshechho jyotirmoy . . .' or 'O anather nath . . .' or 'Bahir pathe bibagi hiya . . .' rang over these prayer meetings, those thrilling notes sung by some of the most famous names in the world of music today. Till I die I do not think I will ever forget the profound majesty of those prayers.

After that, we went to our respective classes: the Kala Bhavan students went one way and the Path Bhavan students the other. As soon as everyone settled in, it was as if the chattering birds had come home to roost and a silence descended over the Ashram.

Then, a gong sounded and the lessons of the day would start.

Gurupalli

Bisected by a dusty red path, the vast fields of the Ashram had a cluster of cottages on one side, known as Gurupalli. These housed our teachers. The cottages stood like dolls' houses in a row framed by tall palm trees and fragrant malatilata creepers. They were modest huts, really, with red-tiled roofs and homely interiors that matched their simple exteriors. Yet, like the people who lived there, they exuded a warmth and a welcoming spirit that drew us to them. The 'furniture' was often just a wooden divan, covered with neat rolls of bedding, and a cupboard for books. The inner courtyard doubled up as an open-air kitchen and the tantalizing aroma of fish curry often wafted across the field to tickle our nostrils. We followed the scent and reached its source, to be greeted with an '*Aisho, aisho, ma* [Come, come, child]', and a helping of fish and rice with some delectable pickle would be placed in front of us. If we were lucky, we got some sandesh or palm-jaggery kheer. My mouth still waters at the memory of those al fresco picnic meals.

As far as I can recall, till 1935, Gurupalli had just three pucca houses. Near the pond was the one that belonged to

Dr Dhirendra Mohan Sen, Gurudev's personal secretary, and another that sprawled over a large compound, appropriately named 'Simantika' (Land's End). This belonged to Shri Lalitmohan.

The Ashram pond near these houses doubled up as a swimming pool, and we watched with envy as our Bengali mates cavorted about, swimming and diving like mermaids. To help the rest of us—landlubbers from Uttar Pradesh, Punjab, Sri Lanka, or Sindh and Gujarat—the Ashram appointed Jiwan da to give us swimming lessons. When Jiwan da felt we were not trying hard enough, he would drop us like penguins into the water and wait for us to thrash about before rescuing us. God knows how much water we swallowed, but we did eventually manage to pass our test. On some occasions, when expert swimmers from outside came to give demonstrations, the Ashram pond turned into an Olympic pool. We never clapped for it was strictly forbidden in the Ashram, but said 'sadhu, sadhu' to express our appreciation.

Most of our gurus stayed in Gurupalli. The first of the little cottages was divided into two parts. One half belonged to Bade Pandit ji (as Pandit Hajari Prasad Dwivedi was called), while the other half housed the family of Gosain ji. Next door, in a pucca house of his own, lived Shri Sarojranjan Chaudhuri. He escorted students like us, who could not go home for Puja because of the long and tiresome journey, to see the annual Durga Puja at Shiyuri. His round face was always wreathed in smiles, and his pretty wife, whom we called Mashima (aunt), took us there in their car, a rare treat. I still remember her lovely face: her hair was trained to frame her oval face in little waves and smelt of the perfumed hair oil she used. She also had the longest eyelashes I have ever seen. A huge red vermilion tika graced her brow and the neat parting of her hair had a similar red streak. Her lips were stained red with the juice of the paan she always chewed. After we had been to see the huge Durga idol at the pandal, Saroj Babu would take us for a final treat: a traditional *jatra* play. Before dark, we were taken back to the Ashram and deposited in the hands of our hostel wardens.

All of us who came from Uttar Pradesh had declared the house of Bade Pandit ji our special adda, and whenever hunger pangs hit us (at least once a day) we trotted off in search of sustenance. We ran through their tiny bedroom and descended on his wife (Bhabhi to us), who was to be found in the little kitchen attached to the courtyard at the back. Bhabhi was a simple Bihari soul, and her sweet voice had given a new twist to my name: Gaura. To her I was always 'Gaw-ra'. Her tiny round frame contained immense patience, and if there was nothing else available to feed us hungry hordes, she would place a whole canister of puffed rice to which she added chopped onions and chillies, fresh green coriander, salt and mustard oil. Within minutes, we had licked it clean.

There were seven or eight of us who attended Pandit ji's Hindi classes. I must tell you a little about Pandit ji at this point. You could spot Pandit ji and his long legs and arms from afar. He always wore a loose khadi kurta with a carelessly slung silk shawl, and his classes were like none other in the Ashram. Often, as soon as a few drops of rain fell from the sky, our otherwise strict Pandit ji would give us all leave 'to get wet'. This was an excuse for the rest of the classes to join in, and those unique rainy day 'holidays' were surely a Shantiniketan invention! Any class was free to seek this kind of leave and get soaked in the rain. We ran around the fields, shouting and splashing with joy, singing

Shraboner gogoner gaaye
Bidyut chamakiya jaaye
Kshane, kshane Shorbori shihariya othe, hai . . .

as we danced.

Whether 'Shorbori' trembled or not I do not know, but the Ashram certainly did, with the shouts and shrieks that we added as we sang these immortal lines.

Apart from the holiday to get wet, Pandit ji had invented another kind of holiday for us. Often, he would ask a few chosen students to trot off to the Ashram's lone cooperative store to buy him shaving blades, or soap or something. The errand boys (or girls) were given a small tip at the end of this 'chore'; so, often the entire class offered to perform this onerous duty. Yet, like all easy-going men, Pandit ji was a terror when his temper was roused. Among the simplest students in our class was one Sharan Prasad. One day, Pandit ji caught him sucking an amla stone in his class. For some unknown reason, sucking amla stones was the rage among the students then and our teachers were fed up. Recently, when he caught some stone-crunchers in his class, Pandit ji had yelled: 'Do you come here to crunch those wretched stones or to study? The next time I catch someone doing this, I'll throw you out of the class, understand?'

Has any child ever taken such threats seriously? So we all continued to slyly suck the stones. God knows how poor Sharan Prasad got caught by Pandit ji that day.

'Come here!' Pandit ji commanded him. 'Open your mouth and show me how many stones you have inside it! Hurry up!' Sharan Prasad quickly hid them under his tongue and opened his mouth obediently.

'Ah-ha,' replied Pandit ji. 'You think I am so stupid that I can't see what you have under your tongue, do you? Get out and stay there for the rest of the class.' Then he turned to point at me: 'Look at her,' he told the class. 'She's just come here from the hills and see how quietly and obediently she sits here. And look at the rest of you! Been here for God knows how long and can't sit still for a minute. Shame on all of you!'

My chest swelled with pride as I heard this and I smiled widely, quite forgetting to keep the stones I had in my mouth safe. Out they popped, and one went flying across the class to land neatly at Pandit ji's feet.

He looked nonplussed at first and then gave a huge shout of laughter. I will never forget that generous laughter; it shamed me more than a shout would have.

I remember another scene. We were all sitting with Pandit ji under the sky, and he was reading the *Sundar Kand* of the Ramayana. When his deep baritone read the text out to us, everything seemed so easy that there were no questions to ask. However, there was one textbook in his course—a selection of poems—that nobody (least of all Pandit ji himself) wanted to ever tackle. 'Why do you want me to read you this?' he'd ask. 'Go read it at home.'

'But Pandit ji,' I begged him one day, 'who can we go to if we don't understand something? You have to help us—what will we do in the exams next month?'

'Stupid child,' he shook his head at me. 'What is in it to understand?'

I read out a few lines that had been troubling me. I still remember them: 'Speak, O Koel! Spread some sweetness in my life.'

'Look,' he clicked his tongue impatiently at me. 'We are talking here of a koel, a cuckoo, not a crow. Obviously, it had a sweet voice and that is what must have pleased the poet. Got it? Enough, now vamoose!'

What could I possibly ask after this limpid deconstruction? However, the same Pandit ji became a tyrant when he took lessons in grammar. He would make us slog for hours until the rules were fixed in our minds to his satisfaction.

'If you sleep through this class,' he warned us, 'you'll never be able to write a line. Understand?' Then he turned to me, 'She was like a meek lamb when she came here but look at her now! Don't think for a minute I can't see what mischief you are up to,' he wagged a fat finger at me. 'I'll pull your ears from your jaw one day! I am going to report you to Jayanti today, you watch!'

Thankfully, he never carried out either of these threats. My ears remain intact, and he did not report me to my older sister, Jayanti. And I can proudly say that I remember every bit of the grammar he taught me.

Often, he would invite the whole class to his home to stargaze. 'Go, run, all of you,' he'd dismiss us. 'Come after dark to my cottage and we'll hold a class there.' I don't know how teachers would react to such unorthodox methods and timetables today, but we loved these impromptu classes. Like the enchanted children behind the Pied Piper of Hamelin, we followed our gurus everywhere they asked us to go. That is why I cannot understand why we hear of demonstrations against teachers and, worse, cheating at exams or threats to stab teachers unless they stepped down. Perhaps the definition of a guru was different in our times.

What can never change, though, is the memory of those mobile classes and those magical hours we spent stargazing with Pandit ji. He pointed out the stars to us, and one constellation after another took shape before our eyes. 'There is the Big Bear,' he said, tracing a circle with his thumb on a palm. He called it Sapt Rishi—the Seven Sages of Heaven.

'Where, Pandit ji?' piped up someone.

'*Arrey*, this idiot Kusum can't see her own nose on her face. There, you ass!' he would point it out again.

Then he showed us the Milky Way, calling it Akash Ganga, the magical river of stars in the sky. My little son recently told me how the Nainital Observatory had acquired the latest telescope. 'You know how huge it is?' he tried to tell me. I nearly laughed as I watched him struggle to explain. How could I puncture his earnest enthusiasm by telling him that the 'telescope' that had revealed the night sky to us was better than the best money could buy. As Pandit ji pointed out one constellation after another, we were convinced that all the stars shining in the sky bowed as they introduced themselves to us and became our friends for life. We had no telescopes or complicated instruments, just one crazy astronomer whose deep voice and expressive hands described the world of stars to us. Lost in the vastness of the sky and Pandit ji's stories, we often lost track of time and only remembered that we were hungry when we heard the gong chime out the summons for dinner.

The next scene: a grammar class with Pandit ji. Once, he brought Tagore's new novel, *Chaar Adhyaay*, to class and read it aloud to us over several days. One day, he came across the line: '*Deke ano Balukdangar Pandit Hajari Prasad ke* [Go and fetch Pandit Hajari Prasad from Balukdangar, the kindergarten]' and guffawed over it for a long time. And now I must tell you about Pandit ji's guffaw. Just as a jeweller knows the difference between a genuine and a cultured pearl, I can tell a heartfelt guffaw from a polite titter. The true guffaw rings out over a room and flows from the heart like a natural waterfall. And, like it, it sprays all who stand near it with joy. Pandit ji had that kind of pure laugh. Perhaps it has changed now, but as far as I know, a true pearl does not age. His whole body would shake with mirth when he laughed. When his laughter floated over the Ashram, it spread a smile on every face. Since our classes were held in the open, every head would turn towards his class at the sound of Pandit ji's guffaw. It was as if a multitude of bells tied to a single string were set in motion and a ripple of happiness ran through the entire Ashram.

'So, Kamla,' he said one day to a student, 'I saw your brother wearing a red *langot* [loincloth] and exercising at dawn today,' and roared with laughter. The rest of us joined him, tickled to death at the thought of someone in a red loincloth doing his morning workout.

Pandit ji once decided to grow a beard, and all of us got after him. '*Chhi*, Pandit ji! It is disgusting. You look like some sadhu baba—you'll have to get rid of it.' Poor Pandit ji tried to tell us that he had boils on his face that made shaving painful but no one was ready to listen. I smile as I remember how easy it was to bully him.

And this was a man who was regarded a colossus in his field. I wonder what he made of this spoilt class that argued with him on the merits of a beard.

~

There was one teacher whose temper we dreaded and that was our English teacher, Tanmay da. I think none of us who ever sat in one of his classes will ever forget him. He was related to Abanindranath Tagore by marriage and the Ashram was full of tales of his fearful temper and strict bearing. He had a round face and wore a faded orange pashmina shawl over his shoulders. His glistening forehead was visible from afar, and as soon as we heard him approach, even the naughtiest boys in the class sat down like meek lambs. On entering the class, he would narrow his sharp gaze to take an X-ray of all the faces before him. Then he would part his thin lips and start reading. And if, god forbid, anyone yawned, all hell would break loose. This was one act of indifference that Tanmay da never forgave.

'This means,' he would say, 'that your attention is elsewhere. So go out and stay there until you decide to return here and pay attention.'

Not a single day passed when some hapless student or the other was not punished for yawning. There is an awful truth about yawns: they spread by osmosis. Have you ever noticed how if someone starts to yawn, a dozen other faces begin to twitch as well? One day, to my horror, I felt a yawn coming. I quickly put my head down and tried to disguise it by flaring my nostrils so that my mouth would not show it. But do you think this escaped Tanmay da's sharp gaze? At first I did not understand that the barb was aimed at me.

'You all know,' his deep voice intoned, 'that there are two types of yawns: internal and external. The first is a shameless act, open for all to see. The other one is more refined: the yawner tries to hide it, like a deer it darts quick looks around and then swallows it so that no one notices it. Only, this makes the pupils of the eyes dilate and also the nostrils. One of my students here has just given me a splendid example of this kind of yawn. So, don't you all think that I should reward this child?'

By the time I could take all this in, my 'art' had been rewarded. He drew a huge mark of Vishnu on my forehead with a piece of chalk and made me stand and show it to the whole class. For days after that, I was greeted with exaggerated bows by my mischievous and cruel classmates, who called out, 'So how are you today, Vaishnavi ji?'

Another one of his pet peeves was untidy handwriting. Often, he would cross out a whole essay and scrawl 'Rewrite this' across it if it had any scratched-out words or was untidily written. Once, a friend of mine went to him and said, 'But Tanmay da, all I had crossed out was one sentence!'

'So . . .' he told her. 'Suppose I cut off just the nose from your pretty face, would you still consider yourself as pretty?'

She slunk away quietly.

~

The Ashram offered a number of interesting locations for holding classes. Our teachers had the option of holding a class under the shade of a perfumed creeper, or in an arbour of the Lata Kunj. There was the horseshoe-shaped bower of flowers, or the dark and verdant Amrakunj (the Mango Grove). Only, Tanmay da had decided that his class would always be held in the small clearing in front of the nursery section, Shishu Vibhag. Rain or shine, he would not move from this spot. Sometimes gentle raindrops fell on our shoulders like the hand of a friend beckoning us to come and play; at other times one could sense a furious thunderstorm brewing, the sort that uprooted trees. But there was nothing that would move Tanmay da to dismiss his class. His orange shawl was like the red flag a guard waves to indicate danger.

'It's started to rain, Tanmay da,' someone once dared to say.

'So?' he answered. 'Are you made of paper that you'll melt?'

Even the raindrops ran away after they heard that reprimand.

'If you really wish to master the English language,' he was fond of telling us, 'then read Dickens.'

Charles Dickens was his favourite novelist, and when he read us passages from *David Copperfield*, *A Christmas Carol* or *Pickwick Papers*, all of us stopped shuffling impatiently. Often, the time for another class came and went unnoticed by us. When I think of how our teachers managed to hold our attention and how pleasant they made the whole process of learning, my eyes well up with gratitude for the opportunity to have attended such a magical school.

The complete antithesis of Tanmay da was Prabhat da. His olive skin, elegant French beard, aristocratic nose and regal bearing were what first attracted us to him. And then there was his 100-watt smile and warm greeting: 'Hey, young lady!' or 'How are you today, little princess?' Tell me, who would not love a teacher who brought such charm when he entered a class? Like Tanmay da, he also had a fixed location: the horseshoe-shaped space under the shade of a maulsari tree in front of the Ashram guest house. A dirt path ran close to this spot and often, a Santhal tribal would pass by playing a haunting tune on his flute. At other times, the birds that lived in the maulsari tree would start up a noisy conference. In any case, that tree supported so much life that it was a constant source of distraction. One day, one of my classmates, bored with the day's lesson, was intently watching some squirrels run up and down a branch. Prabhat da quietly walked up to him and stood there, trying to figure out what was absorbing this student. Of course, the culprit was quite unaware of this development.

'So, my dear Viswamitra,' asked the amiable Prabhat da, 'is your Menaka going to descend from heaven today?'

The whole class burst into laughter and the poor boy blushed to the roots of his hair. Prabhat da was the Ashram's oldest teacher and his treasury of anecdotes could keep us enthralled for hours. His restless hands moved constantly as he taught us history. The truth was that he taught us everything but history in his class. He was a one-man theatre and his stories about great moments from the past were mesmerizing. Occasionally, he would burst into song as he recalled some great dance performance he had seen at the Ashram and tell us how when Gauri di had once danced the audience forgot to say 'sadhu, sadhu' at the end of the performance because they were literally struck dumb! All of us followed him into that glorious past. Then, suddenly, as he was reminded of his duties as a history teacher, he would drag us back to the history lesson he was supposed to teach us that day. This used to remind me of the cowherd in our hills, who played haunting tunes on his flutes as he grazed his flock, and got lost in their music. On becoming aware that his herd had strayed, the poor man would hurriedly put away the enchanted flute to chase it back into the fold. So, after taking us to an enchanted past, Prabhat da would return to earth with the same old William Bentinck reforms with which he had started the day's lesson.

It seemed to us that he needed no textbook because he knew all the dates by heart. This is why he was later decorated with the Rabindra Puraskar for excellence in teaching. Which Indian schoolchild will not shudder at the memory of the dates of the three battles of Panipat? And what about the unending litany of dates that mark the occasions when Mahmud Ghazni attacked us? I don't know about you but I always forgot the year of the French Revolution just when I needed to remember it the most—but Prabhat da rattled them all off as if he had an invisible calendar hanging in front of his eyes. He must have been about fifty years old then but still looked like a young man. A few years ago when I wrote to him after a trip to the USSR, I was stunned to see how firm and steady his hand had remained. I am convinced that like the dates he never faltered over, he remembers each and every student who passed through his hands.

~

The Ashram also had a modest laboratory for the science students, presided over by the genial Pramath da, while the health science and hygiene classes were conducted by the Ashram's 'Daktar Babu'. What we learned from him went far beyond what he taught us in his classes. 'Why would anyone want to know about the coils of a human brain or the twists of a ribcage?' he asked us. 'Don't waste your time learning all this here. Go home and swot it from your textbooks,' he advised us affably.

'Then please, Daktar Babu,' the class piped up, 'sing us a song.'

This was exactly the nudge our Daktar Babu needed. He'd shut the book in front of him with a decisive snap, close his eyes and begin to hum. What a voice God had blessed him with! With a hand cupped over one ear, Daktar Babu launched into our favourite song:

> Kolkata kebol bhule bhara
> Mari hai re . . .

> [Kolkata is a maze,
> I'm in love with it . . .]

As the rest of us clapped to keep time, he warmed up:

> Bou bajaare giya dekhi Bouti kothai nei.
> Shyam Bajare giya dekhlam
> Na Shyam na Rai . . .

> [I went to the bazaar of bahus
> And found no bahu there.

Went on to Shyam Bazar
Found neither Shyam nor Radha . . .]

The wan faces of the sick people in the infirmary would light up as Daktar Babu's jolly voice sang on, for what he could not cure with medicines, Daktar Babu healed with his magical voice. Once he started to sing the famous folk songs of Bengal—*bhatiyali*, *baul* and *kirtan*—he forgot everything, even the fact that the class was over and it was time for us to leave. Our singing doctor could be heard late into the night, warbling away as he cycled his way to some sick patient on the campus. He and I would often have friendly arguments over his pronunciation of Hindi words in the songs he sang but our common love of music always resolved these with laughter. At the time of the annual picnic, we begged him to come along but as he was the only doctor in the Ashram, he couldn't very well leave his patients. However, Daktar Babu resolved this dilemma by coming along anyway, and once he sat down to sing, no one could prise him from his *mridang*. Often, he was joined by our Sanskrit teacher, Gosain ji. Watching them, in their simple homespun dhotis, and listening to their joyous duet in action, one could be misled into thinking that here was a pair of rustic village singers attending a tribal Paush fair. Yet the first beat on the mridang sent a shiver of delight through the audience and a cascade of Chandidas's verses would fill the air:

Prabhate uthiya
Je mukh herinu
Din jaabe aaji bhalo
Kahe Chandidas . . .

After this overture came a scintillating alaap. Never, in all the years that I knew Daktar Babu, did he ever lose that air of joy and sweetness. He went happily wherever he was summoned to help. A scene floats before my eyes: a famous Calcutta football team has arrived to play at the Ashram. The air is filled with the dust raised by the robust players. Suddenly, there is a shout: 'He's broken it, he's broken it . . .' and tearing his way to the injured player is our Daktar Babu, ready to plaster the fractured arm (or leg). There is a cross-country race on and the runners are covered with sweat while running, a kerchief with glucose clamped in their mouths. Suddenly, one of them falls in a dead faint. Daktar Babu peddles his way on his trusty bicycle to the scene of action and is there once again to help.

Whether it was the dreaded cerebral malaria of the Birbhum area, a raging viral epidemic or whatever, Daktar Babu would somehow manage to pull his patients out of the jaws of death. In all the years that I was at the Ashram, there were just two incidents where he lost this battle. Once when the popular Kala Bhavan student Durga Ray lay critically ill, pleading with his burning eyes to deliver him from raging fever. Durga Ray died despite Daktar Babu's best efforts. And the other time was when a young student from Uttar Pradesh, Harishankar, drowned in the Ashram pool. I still remember Daktar Babu's helpless gestures, furiously feeling for Harishankar's pulse, blowing air into his lifeless lungs and then shaking his head in disbelief and horror.

Those days, our Ashram did not have a lady doctor and Daktar Babu was our only messiah. From Bhubandanga to Shriniketan, and from the neighbouring Santhal villages to Bolpur, Daktar Babu peddled his way on his trusty bike, smiling and singing his way cheerfully from one patient's bedside to another. Our Ashram had among its students the princes of Tripura and Sumatra–Java; the scions of some of the wealthiest industrialists came there, as did princesses from Agartala and Assam. All of them held out their wrists for Daktar Babu to feel their pulse and surrendered meekly to his bitter medicines. For him, whether your blood was blue or red, you were a sick person in need of tender loving care.

'Show me your tongue,' he'd say. 'Hunh! Call this an illness? Go, have a dose of *panchtikt* and a bowl of good fish broth. You'll be as right as rain tomorrow! Next . . .'

Most of us tried to run away before we were made to swallow that deadly panchtikt! It was pure poison, I tell you. But there was no escaping it for it was Daktar Babu's favourite medicine; a palliative for all ills of the human system. He had devised its special formula himself and cured most of us with just one dose of it. Even now, when I recall its bitter taste, my body shivers in disgust. All of us were made to stand in a row and the bitter concoction shoved down our unwilling throats.

Fish was regularly cooked in the Ashram kitchen and Daktar Babu knew which fish was good for which ailment. 'Have magur fish for good eyesight,' he'd declare, 'and hilsa for the brains. Get rid of a cough with shukto and have chingri to deal with asthma.' Often, students like us who had never had fish before would go to him to dislodge a fishbone from our throat. He made you swallow a whole banana and stuff it down until your eyes nearly popped out of your head. 'See?' he'd declare triumphantly at the end of the ordeal. 'Gone, isn't it? It's gone to your stomach now and there's no need to worry. The stomach has a larger opening than your throat, understand? Next time, eat fish more carefully, stupid child!'

I have never been able to fathom how he kept his life so uncomplicated—there was a childlike innocence about every aspect of his life, whether his rumpled clothes or his smile. Believe me, even clothes stitched in Savile Row would not be so long remembered as his home-washed shirt, or his cloth jacket topped with a battered sola topi on his head. I wonder what he looks like now! Today, when it appears as if the green paddy fields, the Santhal villages, those shady glens and groves, the little sparkling stream we called Kopai, took one almighty turn and changed their hues forever, is it possible that Daktar Babu has held on to his colours? Last year, I got a postcard from him saying, 'I am an old man now . . .', and the spidery letters brought his dancing fingers joyously beating a mridang before my eyes. He must be well over seventy by now, and his wife, I heard, was bedridden after a paralytic stroke. I can't picture our Messiah as an old and trembling man; all I want to remember is that smiling face and those sparkling eyes.

The Ashram's 'hospital' was an old building situated at its very edge. Like the rest of the Ashram, it exuded a serenity that beckoned, rather than repelled, patients. That modest hospital was the only one I have ever known that did not reek of the sickening smell of medicines and fear. Large windows on its walls brought in light and sunshine and were a means of cross-ventilation as well. The walls were adorned with cheerful frescoes and on the far horizon was a railway track with a signal that was endlessly entertaining for the patients as they gazed out. Next door, another little room doubled up as Daktar Babu's office and his dispensary. Daktar Babu's faithful companion was the compounder, whom we knew as Yadav Babu, who handled everything from compounding mixtures to taking down patients' histories. Often, this little room became a classroom where Daktar Babu taught his students while keeping an eye on a sick patient.

What a strange classroom it was indeed. On one side lay the weighing scales and on the other was an examination table neatly covered with a red blanket. Two dead snakes were preserved in glass jars with chemicals. Also in the room was a skeleton in a cupboard and it leered at us from there as Daktar Babu taught us anatomy. One day, a classmate said that it was actually a Santhal tribal's skeleton that Daktar Babu had bought from one of the tribal villages nearby. All of us were goggle-eyed at this revelation but no one had the courage to verify this. Ultimately, I offered to bell the cat. Prodded by my friends, I got up and asked: 'Daktar Babu, is it true that this skeleton belongs to a Santhal tribal?'

'Ah, o ho!' Daktar Babu pondered over this seriously. 'Wait, I think I'll verify it from the skeleton himself. Let's see what the good creature has to say.' Then, equally seriously, he turned to the skeleton and asked its skull loudly: 'Excuse me, sir, were you a Santhal? This girl would like to know.'

Then he turned to me and said: '*Baap re baap*, he says— write this down quickly, girl, for the person who answers this question correctly will top the class!' The whole class was rocking with laughter by now and Daktar Babu, for the first and perhaps only time, cuffed my ear and said: 'The next time I hear a stupid question from you, out you go! Understand?'

That evening, still smarting from the humiliation of that episode, I was slowly walking back to the hostel when I felt a kind hand on my shoulder. 'Is your ear really hurting, child? But don't you dare repeat such foolishness ever again.'

Daktar Babu and I were friends once again.

I don't think any of us will ever forget our Daktar Babu. He is inscribed forever, like the gurgling stream Kopai, and his song, like the stream's gurgle, rings even now in our ears: '*Kolkata ek bhul bhulaiya re . . .*'

~

We had two Hindi teachers: Shri Bhagwati Prasad Chandola and Mohanlal Vajpayee.

Tall, fair and rather forbidding, Chandola ji was among the strictest teachers in the Ashram. He would not tolerate any noise or indiscipline in the classroom. The minute he felt matters were getting out of hand, he snapped shut the book in front of him and retreated into a hurt silence that stretched and stretched until all of us begged for his forgiveness. He used this weapon of silence like a whip to crack over our heads on several occasions and each time, he won.

Our other Hindi teacher was a merry old soul and, like so many of our teachers in the Ashram, a great musician. In fact, he was my music teacher. I cannot even remember how many of Ghalib's ghazals and Bundelkhandi folk songs, such as the *phaag*, I learnt from him. He would sing and I'd jot down the words and notations:

Aa jaungi badi bhor
Dahiya leke
Aa jaungi badi bhor

Na mano chunri dhari rakho
Motiyan lagi kor
Dahiya leke

While Vajpayee ji was lost in the lines of this thumri, his students waited patiently for him to come back to the lesson in front of him.

There was another singing guru in the Ashram: Acharya Kshiti Mohan Sen. His granddaughter, Sunipa, was my friend, and I often went across to their home with her. Kshiti Mohan Babu's gentle face would light up at the sight of the two of us. As I touched his feet, he'd pass a loving hand over my head and ask: 'Another Kabir today?' This was our private joke because often, when asked to sing at an assembly, I would ask him for a Kabir bhajan. 'Give me one that no one has ever heard so far, please,' I'd beg and he would produce one from his vast collection. 'Enough!' he told me once. 'Get hold of another poet now, for God's sake.' But when I sang the Kabir bhajan for him, his eyes filled up with emotion. 'You'll earn a great name for yourself one day, child,' he had said. Sadly, this was one prophecy that I was never able to fulfil. My life took me very far away from my music after I left the Ashram.

However, I still remember those verses I learnt from him. In fact, I can see him—his eyes shut in pleasure, his large body wrapped in a silk shawl, and his feet in wooden clogs, keeping the beat as I sing:

Jhari lage mahiliya
gagan ghaharaye
Sunnmahal se

Amrut barse
Prem anand hvaiy sadhu anhaye
Jhari lage . . .

Every Wednesday at the morning assembly, his deep baritone
would recite these majestic words:

Andhkar theke amader aalote niye jao tomar je dokhin mukh
tamaso maa jyotirgamaye . . .

Those words swirled over our heads like the sound of thunder
over mountain caves to resonate for a long time.

~

Gosain ji had taught me Sanskrit when I was in Path Bhavan,
the school section of the Ashram, but he remained a part of my
life beyond it. His love and fathomless knowledge of classical
music were a perennial source of learning. So whether it
was any question related to a problem in music or a better
understanding of Brahmo sangeet, based on the orthodox
Dhrupad style, Gosain ji was my port of call. He would haul
out his pakhawaj and play out all the complicated rhythmic
patterns that kept the beat at rehearsals. I can never forget the
joy on his face as his hands beat out the deep sounds of the
pakhawaj to accompany us.

His young son, Viru, a happy little boy, had died at a
tragically early age while we were there. He was Gosain
ji's only child, and a motherless one to boot. Gosain ji was
heartbroken and his grief was visible to all of us who went to

pay our condolences. I can still see the body of his beloved child laid out on the floor and a shocked Gosain ji sitting next to it. Consoling him was his neighbour and dear friend, Pandit Hajari Prasad Dwivedi, whose own eyes were streaming with tears.

There is no grief to surpass the pain of losing one's child, I think. However, Gosain ji pulled himself out of it by turning to his teaching and beloved music. Many years later, he married again and had a beautiful daughter. Gosain ji's second wife was a pretty young woman and would sometimes hand over the little girl to me, saying, 'Here, take Khuku for a little while and I'll quickly wash some clothes.'

'But, Bou di,' I'd protest, 'I have a class and that too with Gosain ji. He'll be furious if I'm late.'

'So? Just tell him you were looking after his daughter, that's why you're late,' she solved the problem in her inimitable way. I followed her advice and it worked!

All I can say of the special relationship that we had with all our teachers in the Ashram is that to them we were one of their own. Similarly, we looked at them as elders in our own family; so, running errands for Pandit ji, babysitting for harried mothers or stitching buttons on a shirt for another teacher—all these were ways of bringing us closer to the lessons they taught us in class.

~

Moshai was our geography teacher and, like so many other teachers, he also lived in the Ashram. His daughter, Supriya (Tultul to us), and his son, Vaman, were both in class with

me. We were all in awe of their father because his temper
was legendary. If you were unable to answer a question he
asked, he'd turn those fearful eyes on you and then yank you
up by your braid: 'Devi, did you forget to learn your lesson?'
And it wasn't just us girls with plaits and braids who suffered
this yanking; the boys were pulled up by their hair as well. I
remember once a whole tuft of hair came off in his hands after
he pulled up one of the boys in our class. His own son, Vaman,
was one of the most mischievous boys in the Ashram—he
was short and had a high-pitched treble. Once, after he was
yanked by his father, he was held up as an example of what
would happen if the rest of us ever tried to hoodwink Moshai.

When he lost his temper, it made no difference to Moshai
whether his daughter stood in front of him or his son. There
was a rule against corporal punishment in the Ashram but
Moshai had his own interpretation of this convention. He
would pull an offending student's hair so hard that he often
managed to pull a few hairs out of the skull. '*Devi, padhashuno
kore asho nai, bolo to Newcastle kothai*?]Devi, it appears you
haven't done your work today. Tell me, where is Newcastle?]'
I wasn't able to answer him that day and he twisted my ear so
hard that it hurt me for days. Many years later, when I visited
Newcastle, my ear began to hurt on its own. However, he was
a totally different person at home. The little cottage where
he stayed had a thatched roof and the only 'furniture' was a
wooden *takhat*, with big fat bolsters against which the portly
Moshai reclined, bare-chested.

When he saw me, he'd rise and call out to his children,
'Come here and see who's arrived. Bring something nice to eat
because I pulled her ears really hard today.' And then would

arrive a delicious array of home-made sweets and snacks like coconut and jaggery laddoos and I'd forget all the pain of the afternoon ear-pull.

~

Anil Chanda was Gurudev's secretary for years, and later became our political science teacher when we entered college. He took a deep interest in all the activities of the Ashram. Anil da and his wife, Rani di, became very close to us because they, along with their son, Abhijit, and Anil da's brother, Suhas, would often come to Almora and stay with us. Several nephews and nieces of his clan were students of the Ashram as well. His house, called Konark, was a favourite refuge for hungry students, and the charming Rani di would produce dainty fish cutlets, or a tasty pickle to be smeared on paper-thin chapatis. No one ever returned hungry from that hospitable home. Later, Anil da moved to Delhi and stayed on there.

Anil da was always put in charge of all our excursions. I remember two such trips with him: one to Rajmahal and another to Banaras.

When we went to Banaras, Anil da had arranged for us to stay at Rajghat School. The next day, we roamed all around town with him, went on a boat ride on the Ganga and even had the town's famous chaat. Yet, we still wanted more, especially a tonga ride through the atmospheric lanes around Viswanath Temple. So we took the awfully dangerous step of playing hooky and sneaking off on a private excursion by ourselves. We managed to summon a tonga without anyone's knowledge and after a sheet was rigged around it as a purdah, we set off. We were pretty sure that since Anil da had just deposited us back, he was unlikely to send for us for another few hours—and that was all the time we needed for this stolen trip. But the best-laid plans of man are always upset by you-know-who. We had a great time, roaming through those magical lanes, going to bangle-sellers' stalls, eating delicious kachoris, buying saris. Finally, after stuffing our mouths with the famed Banarasi paan, we turned to go back. 'We must be back before six,' we told the tonga driver. 'And mind you stop the tonga before we reach the school!' we warned him. He nodded vigorously and trotted off, only to stop a few minutes later. There, in front of us, were the locked gates of a railway crossing.

After what seemed like hours to us, a slow-moving freight train arrived and died just before it could clear the gates. There was no hope of the gates opening for a long time, we realized, so we all confabulated and decided that the only solution was to take a longer route back. We would have to beg for Anil da's forgiveness but we could cross that bridge when we came to it. But, as soon as our tonga driver turned, there stood Anil da. I still shudder when I remember the anger on his face. He said nothing there and paid off the tonga driver. Then he turned to us. 'Aren't you ashamed of yourselves?' he thundered. 'You are students of the Ashram and I am responsible for you! What would I have done if that tonga driver had run away with you girls?'

We stood there with bowed heads, like ducks quivering before a hunter, for none of us had the gumption to even raise our eyes and face him. Later, of course, we managed to placate him. He then told us that when he came looking for us and was told that we had gone off to the Viswanath Temple lanes, his blood ran cold.

Who had told him of our plans, we wondered, until we realized that one of the students of the school we were staying in was the culprit. The 'student' was actually a Pandit from Mathura, much older than us, and most odd. He used to wear a dhoti-kurta, topped with a bright red waistcoat, and always had a flower stuck in his buttonhole. The moment we saw him, we would start to giggle, and someone would say, 'Here comes the red engine and his searchlight!' Instead of being put off, Pandit ji would flash us a grateful smile for taking note of him. This made him a terrific butt of our jokes. 'Arrey, Pandit ji,' someone would call out, 'just run and fetch us a paan.' Someone else would say, 'Fetch us some chamchams, please, Pandit ji.' And he would reply, 'Of course, at once,' and dash off, only to return later, covered in perspiration from his chores, with our requests held in his outstretched hands. When he saw us getting the sheet fixed over the tonga that afternoon, someone told him, 'Don't tell anyone that we are off to the Viswanath Temple area, all right?'

Pandit ji was delighted to be the keeper of our secret and bent over to indicate his assent. 'Go happily,' he blessed us. 'I will keep guard here until you all return.' His anxious pacing up and down was probably what had alerted Anil da, who had been on his way to his room when he spotted him. Anil da called out to Pandit ji, 'What is it, man? Have the girls asked you to fetch something from the market again?'

'Oh no!' replied our truthful secret-keeper. 'They have gone there secretly in a tonga and I am waiting here for them to come back before they are discovered.'

~

A few years ago, when I visited the Ashram, I discovered that Rani di now lived all alone in their rambling house. Where else could she go after Anil da's death? A garland of wilted flowers was draped over a huge framed photograph of her husband. Rani di followed my gaze with sad eyes. There were no helpers or servants to dust and clean, she seemed to tell me silently.

'Abhijit works on a tea plantation,' she said. 'His son was with me for a few years when he was studying here, now he has also gone away. I'm now almost crippled with arthritis and on top of this is the ever-present danger of the Naxalites around us. *Shona amar, beche aachi, bujhli*? [My dear child, I'm waiting to go, understand?]'

Rani di was summoned by Tagore to look after him in his last days. Many recall Anil da and his contribution to the intellectual life of the Ashram, but only some of us know how much of that was due to Rani di's warmth and caring hospitality.

I lowered my eyes to hide from her tears and mine. Anil da and Rani di used to be the power couple of their time, their home the centre of intellectual soirees and music concerts. All visiting artists, musicians and foreign dignitaries to the Ashram were entertained by them. These rooms once rang with laughter and music. To see them reduced to dusty caverns was unbearable.

~

One occupant of Gurupalli who was not a teacher was Shri Lalitmohan Gupta. Yet he was a guru of another kind. His elder daughter, Parul, was married to Gurudev's private secretary at that time, Dr Virendramohan Sen. The middle daughter, Anima, was a student with us, and the third, Nilima, was then in the nursery section of the Ashram. Today, she is a well-known exponent of Rabindra sangeet. We would often arrive at Lalitmohan Babu's home to ask for his help in writing an essay, or to have a difficult lesson explained while his wife would hand out delicious sweets from her cupboard: chandrapuli, gvaja, chamcham, kheerer sandesh. And whenever I went, she managed to get some fish fried specially for me. I passed some of my most memorable times seated on a cool mat in their home, Simantika. Lalitmohan Babu was a devoted acolyte of Gandhiji and I would often find him sitting near his wife's bedside (she was often unwell) patiently turning a charkha. 'You must have been a Bengali in your previous birth, child,' he'd often say to me. 'Look at the way she relishes a fish-head and chana dal!' he'd tell his wife.

While Lalitmohan Babu said this as an appreciation of my fondness for all things Bengali, my critics have made this a target to find fault with my work. 'What is Shivani's great style all about?' they scoff. 'All she has is the lyrical romanticism of Bengal in her pen!' Whenever such comments reach me, I recall Lalitmohan Babu saying fondly, 'You must have been a Bengali in your previous birth, child . . .'

~

One of the most feared occupants of Gurupalli was Maulana Alimuddin Sahib, who used to live in the house opposite Simantika. Stern of visage, he always wore a fez cap, loose pyjamas and a long robe. 'Maulana Sahib, salaam,' we'd say, and he would scowl at us in return. Fed up of his rough behaviour, we resorted to teasing him and decided to play a prank on him. If I had not been so fleet of foot then, Maulana Alimuddin's broom would surely have thwacked my back that day!

Maulana Sahib had once gone on a long leave to Dacca and someone spread a rumour that he had married a beautiful girl there and brought her home as his new begum. No one had seen her but they swore that she was like a houri. What a glowing complexion she had and what eyes! they raved. Someone claimed to have spotted half a dozen silken burqas on the Maulana's clothes line one day, while someone had seen her slender wrist jingling with green bangles as she threw out the garbage another day from behind a half-open door. Naturally, we were dying to see her for ourselves but never caught so much as a glimpse of anyone outside the Maulana's house. Eventually, I volunteered to do something about it.

There was a large garbage bin outside the Maulana's back door, I recalled. If I could climb it, I might be able to catch a glimpse of his elusive begum. It was no joke to climb that bin, mind you, and that too in a sari. Somehow, I hitched up my sari, managed to clamber on it and then swung dangerously from the skylight. All I could see was an empty room, with a few discarded lungis strewn around. The only occupant of the room seemed to be the Maulana, who was sweeping the dusty floor with a broom. Suddenly, I lost my footing as the rope of the skylight gave way, and the sound of my frantic scrabbling drew the Maulana's attention. He caught just a glimpse of someone hanging from the skylight and ran to catch the intruder but I was faster than him on my feet. I ran and hid in Simantika next door and stayed there until the Maulana went back to his room. Never again, I swore, would I ever try to snoop around his dreaded home.

One last episode regarding the Maulana must be recorded here before I turn my attention elsewhere. Pandit Hajari Prasad Dwivedi once invited the Maulana to speak on Hadith at a literary meeting. The problem was how to record the proceedings. Pandit ji solved this in a unique way. 'Don't worry,' he laughed. 'I'll manage it.' He did so by composing eight Sanskrit slokas that captured the essence of the Maulana's performance.

I can still recall the opening lines composed by Pandit ji as minutes of that memorable lecture:

Sadya snana samapnantar dhyutprodbhasi kaka
Diptim   choran   tatparam   navtaram   topi
vahannamundhyamyasau
Kinchindhrura vatpraroha jatilam dhadhi samabhedhyan
Maulana Alimuddin sahib vado haddisamakhyatvan . . .

[Displaying a new black cap upon his skull,
A cap that would easily steal the glow from a crow's hastily washed feathers,

Pulling his fingers through a beard,
Tangled like the hanging roots of a Banyan tree,
Maulana Alimuddin Sahib delivered
a discourse on Hadith]

~

And now I must recall a few other teachers from Gurupalli, because without their presence my memoir of the Ashram can never be considered complete.

Sri Shailajaranjan Majumdar, Shantimoy Ghosh and Indira Debi—all of them taught me music. Shailaj da was short, fair and blessed with a charming childish gurgle of a laugh. I do not recall ever seeing him lose his temper. His music was his life—he would fit his neck into the curve of the israj, shut his eyes in concentration and sing out each line to teach us. Often, he would place a book of notations in front of us, saying: 'Look at this line: it is not sung in a flat line, but like this . . .' Perhaps this is why we never forgot a single note taught by him. I can wager that all of us who learnt our Rabindra sangeet from him can never deviate from the original scores. Even more enjoyable than learning from him was listening to him. I recently heard 'Krishnakali aami tarei boli . . .' and was instantly transported back in time to that magical occasion when we all heard it sung for the first time by Shailaj da in the presence of Gurudev himself.

Kaalo? Ta she jotoi
kaalo hok
Dekkhechhi taar
kaalo harin chokh . . .

The years have not dimmed the brilliance of that voice.

Indira Debi would conduct the rehearsals for songs sung on special occasions in the Ashram. Chaudhurani Indira Debi, to give her full title, was Tagore's own niece and renowned all over Bengal for her beauty. Her Mughal profile had led Tagore to nickname her 'Bibi', because she reminded him of a Mughal princess. And indeed, she had a patrician Mughal profile, with her longish face, smooth, unlined skin and carefully coiffured hair that fell in waves over her broad forehead. As for the saris she wore, they were so beautiful that we often got distracted by their weaves and colours and forgot to sing! She would place one upturned palm on a knee and keep the beat with the other, as she introduced us to the intricacies of the complex rhythmical patterns of Indian classical music. She told us of the difference in the rhythms of Brahmo music and compared it to the classical notations of orthodox north Indian music. It was thus that we learnt the Western system of musical notations and the fact that marrying the two into a unique form was the work of Tagore's father, Maharishi Debendranath Tagore, who used the Dhrupad as the inspiration for Brahmo sangeet. This is perhaps why even Tagore was always partial to the Dhrupad as a musical form.

I can still see her, lost in ecstasy, singing:

Tare aart kare
Chandra tapan
Dev manav vande charan . . .

or

Ja hariye jaaye
Ta aagle bashe
raee bekat aar . . .

We learnt Indian classical music as well as Rabindra sangeet at the Ashram. In addition, for those who were interested in dance there were classes on Manipuri and Kathakali conducted by brilliant teachers. Shanti da went to Kandy in Ceylon and brought back the dance forms of that fascinating island. In the same way, Mrinalini Sarabhai (then Swaminathan) went to Java, and Tagore used the dance style she brought back in several dance dramas later. The first time Kathakali was performed in the Ashram, it was by the young Asha Ojha, then a new entrant to the Ashram. I even remember the song, '*Maya bono n biharini horini, gohon swapno shoncharini . . .*'

A chest kept in Kala Bhavan used to store the exotic costumes worn for these dances. There were crowns, huge earrings, ankle bells and countless other such treasures to be found inside it. The make-up was generally handled by Gauri di (the artist Nandalal Bose's daughter-in-law). I remember once she made my foster sister Mohini into such a credible Pathan that even I could not recognize her! As it is, Mohini was tall and blindingly fair, with a Grecian nose to die for. When she came on to the stage, the audience whispered among themselves to ask, 'Who is this? Has Gurudev brought a Pathan from Bolpur today?' At the end of such performances, we were all treated to a feast, presided over by Sarojini di, who went around with a huge bowl of rasagullas and gave each actor a special pat with an extra helping as she congratulated them on their part that day. We used to call Sarojini di 'Annapurna' (the Goddess of Plenty).

Sarojini di's association with the Ashram went back a long way. When her only child, Ronen, died suddenly, leaving behind a young wife, Gurudev called her to the Ashram and handed over to her the supervision of the Ashram's kitchen so that she could forget her sorrow and work with young people. A few months after she came to Shantiniketan from her home in Shriniketan, her daughter-in-law gave birth to a lovely daughter, Smriti. Sadly, Smriti was just five years old when she lost her life in an accident. Sarojini di went almost mad with grief, yet she did not give up the responsibilities that Gurudev had given her. She still went around the mess each evening, peering into our thalis to see whether we had eaten properly. If ever any one of us fell ill, she would prepare special food in her own kitchen and bring it across. April and May were the worst months in the Ashram, when hot winds blew over the dusty plains of Bengal and the water in the taps was almost boiling, and no matter how much water you drank, your thirst could never be quenched. Sarojini di would get nimbu paani made in huge terracotta urns and forbid us to stir outdoors without a glass of her refreshing lemonade. This is why in all the years that we spent in the Ashram, we never missed our mothers—Sarojini di more than made up for our absent mothers.

In truth, the Ashram was like a vast joint family, joined together not by ties of blood but by love. I still remember the likes and dislikes of my classmates as well as I remember those of my own siblings. Amazingly, even though we had never visited anyone's homes, we were as familiar with each

other's families as if they were our own kith and kin. No
matter that many students there were not even from our own
country, leave alone our region. No one ever giggled at the
shaven heads of the Ashram's Buddhist students, and their
ochre robes, or at those who wore wooden clogs and long
pigtails and studied at Vidya Bhavan. It was as if the generosity
of Tagore's vision oversaw the whole Ashram and blessed us
with his liberal views.

~

The famous film actor Balraj Sahni was also a member of
the staff at the Ashram for a few years. He taught English
literature and his classes were famous for their unorthodox
teaching methods. For instance, he would hand us the
editorial torn out of a newspaper and ask us to write a
precis of it. Or, sometimes, he would read out a short story
that he was writing. Little did we know that his dashing
good looks would one day make him one of India's most
famous film stars. In the Ashram, you could spot him
from afar: a jaunty walk and a red kurta (he was a lifelong
member of the Communist Party). His classes on English
poetry had us entranced because he read poetry like no
one else I've met.

One summer, he came on a visit to Almora and stayed
with us. He was utterly enchanted by an old church near the
house and often walked to it. One day, he picked up an old,
tattered Bible from the derelict building and brought it home.
My mother was not happy about this at all and told me to ask
him to return it. 'God knows who it belonged to,' she added

darkly. 'Such old things often bring bad luck if you take them away from their place.'

I dutifully reported this to Balraj Sahni and he laughed at such superstitious mumbo jumbo. Years later, when his lovely wife, Dammo, passed away at a tragically young age, my mother all but said, 'I told you so.'

His wife, Damayanti—a pretty, curly-haired, bright-eyed young woman—was an inmate of our hostel because the building that they were to stay in was still under construction. I have seldom met anyone who matched her vivacity and joie de vivre. She was quite a bit older, yet preferred to spend most of her time amongst us. Her eyes had a sparkle that nothing could ever dim. Like most Punjabi girls of that time, she wore a salwar kameez of the same colour with a starched dupatta carelessly wrapped around her neck. She would blow into my room like a tornado, fling away the book I was reading and say, 'Listen, bookworm! Is this night meant to be spent with one's eyes glued to a book? Let's go and find a dholak and we'll sing songs in my room! Come, come!'

Who could resist such an invitation? Within a few minutes, like the Pied Piper of Hamelin, she would collect a bunch of us, settle down with her dholak and start a string of songs. As the evening caught fire, she'd wind her dupatta around her head like a turban and start to dance with one of the girls. I can still see her with the dholak clamped between her legs, or with her earrings and necklace flying as she twirled around, singing lustily:

Addhi raati
Chann tare

Parshu pyara ankh mare
Parshurama maththa sadiya
Dil mera jeeta taine

Damayanti died tragically young, but even now, whenever I hear the beat of a dholak, she comes back to my mind.

~

Another fun-loving person there was Kshitish da. He had taught us English grammar when we were in school, and when we reached college, he was our English teacher once more. At picnics, there were few who could rival his vivacity. He was quite a dandy and wore a rakish beret or even a khadi shervani. At the end of our community feasts, it was customary for him to loudly ask: '*Laglo kaimon?* [How was it?]' and for us to scream back as loudly and enthusiastically: '*Besh!* [Wonderful!]' Apart from the Bengali folk songs he sang with gusto, he had a special repertoire of English songs, and often when we were on our way back to the Ashram after a long and happy day spent outdoors, he would start:

Weep no more, my lady, O weep no more today!
We will sing one song for our old Kentucky home
far away
Old Kentucky forever . . .

Our other English teacher was Gurdial Mallik, an affectionate, avuncular figure whom we called 'Chacha ji'. His niece, Kamla, was a dear friend, and because she called him Chacha ji, that is what we all did. He was our port of call in every hour of need and he bailed us out each time. He was like the Ashram's banyan tree whose cool shade gave succour to countless students down the years.

Chacha ji may have been our English teacher, but he was more like a Sufi saint. With his long white beard and the love that shone through his large limpid eyes, he looked like a saint too. He lived like a hermit in an austere cell-like room in Kala Bhavan and all his worldly possessions hung from a rope stretched across the room. And what were they? Khaddar kurta pyjamas and a towel, and books piled up inside a small wooden cupboard. That was all! 'Chacha ji, don't you have a trunk?' we asked one day.

'And why, pray, do I need one?' he shot back. 'Whatever I have hangs here. *Miyan ji ke teen kapre—suttan, nara, bas!* [Miyan ji has three clothes, a pyjama, a drawstring, that's it].'

Every Wednesday, he would lead the prayer at the morning assembly. In a deep voice, when he sang '*Tab sharnayi aayo re thakur, ava mere thakur. Utar gaya mere man ka sanshaya . . .*', a beautiful hymn from the Granth Sahib, there was pin-drop silence, for his voice transported us to a place where all our problems seemed to evaporate.

As I recall him, I also remember with horror a hideous prank we played that could have led to our being expelled from the Ashram had he not come to our rescue. I was a student of the intermediate class then. In those days, the Ashram was affiliated to Calcutta University and we had to go to Vidyasagar College to take our examinations.

That is where I met a beautiful girl called Sandhya. Not only was she beautiful, she was blessed by the goddesses of both learning and wealth. On receiving our exam papers, she would be the first to finish and get up. Her elder sister, Ranga, was the daughter-in-law of one of the city's wealthiest Marwari families, and each day she came to drop and pick her up in a different car. Sandhya's plait swung to her toes. I could go on and on. In short, she was the epitome of everything a young girl wishes to be and have. She once told us the secret of her glowing skin. 'In Burma, where my parents live,' she told us, 'we all have good complexions because we make a paste of sandalwood and rub it into our skin each day.' After that, all of us went in search of sandalwood to make into a paste and rub into our faces as well.

Sandhya's father was a prosperous businessman in Burma who owned a number of rice mills. No wonder she was like a grain of the best basmati rice herself—slender, delicate and fragrant! When she was returning to Burma, she gave me a lovely photograph of herself; 'to remind you of our fleeting friendship', she said. Little did we know then what a huge problem that photograph would create for me one day.

Those days, there was a strict watch over us girl students in the Ashram, following a silly episode regarding a love letter written by a girl student from Africa to a Muslim boyfriend. An illiterate maid had handed it over to our French warden instead and the fallout was visited on all our heads. Each evening, after the five o'clock attendance was taken, our hostel gates were shut and we were barred from going out. Even when my own brother came to visit us, the French warden would peep in four or five times to make sure that all was in order. To pass the unending evenings, one day, a very dangerous plan took birth in our bored heads. There were several students in the Ashram from the Punjab in those days, and they would subscribe to the *Tribune*, then a very popular newspaper. We all were addicted to the coverage of a famous Karachi trial being covered by it at that time. The story, serialized each day, was like an episode from a detective serial and we'd fight with each other to read it first. One day, my eyes fell upon a classified matrimonial advertisement in the paper seeking a beautiful, convent-educated bride for a Western-educated Rajput boy. Caste and dowry was no bar, but beauty was a prerequisite, it declared. I decided that someone so crass deserved a wicked answer. That, I thought, would teach that Western-educated Rajput a lesson or two.

A few like-minded friends supported my silly scheme. I was given the task of writing the letter and my adviser was Kamla Mallik, Sri Gurdial Mallik's niece, known for her proficiency in English. I can tell you that that letter was a work of art—I rate it as my finest literary piece. It said that I was a young and beautiful widow and after that lie, the rest of the letter wrote itself. I was a paragon of beauty, virtue and intelligence. My fictitious widow was of royal lineage, and we were certain that no one in their right senses could reject such a proposal. If I had sent it to a magazine as a story, the editor would have come begging to marry me, I was told. Laced with poetry and syrupy prose, it was finally ready for posting. All my friends applauded my efforts when I read it aloud. But where were we to get a photograph that the wretched Rajput had asked to be sent along with the reply? Sending one of ours was not even an option. That is when I remembered Sandhya, my beautiful Burmese friend. There was not even a remote chance that she could be traced, we thought. What was more, she was truly beautiful. The address we gave for correspondence when posting it was 'Shrimati Gangabai, Shribhavan, Shantiniketan'. Let this Prince Charming come here looking for a Gangabai and our French warden would take care of him, we giggled.

That night, after my giggly friends had departed, I was hit by a panic attack. Suppose he came here and the warden recognized my handwriting? There was another panic attack to follow: my elder sister Jayanti was by then the assistant warden and a model of rectitude. Gurudev had named her 'Bharat Mata' for her devotion to duty and discipline. If she found out about my role in this, she would not hesitate to pull my ears and send me packing. I woke up my friends and their faces went white when I told them of the consequences that could take place. We decided to devise a way in which the Rajput should be prevented from ever coming in search of this fictitious widow.

On the sixth day, our blood ran cold when the warden asked us, 'Who is Gangabai?', waving a letter at us.

'I am,' said Kamla and held out her hand. 'This is my name back home.' We had rehearsed this answer for the last five days. We ran to my room and read the letter behind closed doors. 'I am interested in your daughter's hand,' he had written. 'I am staying at the Grand Hotel in Calcutta and shall be with you the day after tomorrow to discuss this matter.' Two thumping hearts—mine and 'Gangabai's'—almost stopped beating at this point. We were in a right royal soup.

'There is just one way out,' I told Kamla. 'Let's go to Chacha ji and confess our crime. He's the only person who can save us.'

And that is what we did. Our faces were white with fear when we entered his room. 'So what have you two been up to now?' he smiled, as if he already knew what we had done. We told him our story and first he guffawed, then he turned serious. After all, the culprits were his niece and the younger sister of the assistant warden.

'Show me that letter,' he said. He finished reading it, folded it and put it in his pocket. 'Go now, you foolish girls!' he told us. 'You are fortunate that I not only know this boy, but I know his father as well. No one would dare to play such a prank on this family. I'll just call the Grand Hotel and apologize on your behalf. Go and sleep in peace,' he added kindly. 'No one will come here to see Gangabai's daughter,' he twinkled.

God knows how many students he had bailed out. No wonder his favourite hymn (which he often sang in our morning assemblies) was 'Ab sharanayi aayo re Thakur . . . [I have come to your sanctuary, my Lord . . .]'. His deep voice made even the stained glass of the windows tremble.

~

Apart from Chacha ji, the English department had Dr Alex Aronson, Miss Marjorie Sykes and Kshitish Roy. Miss Sykes was a Quaker and a brilliant teacher and she still works at a social service centre in Madhya Pradesh. Dr Aronson is in Israel and Kshitish Roy lives by himself in Shantiniketan. Dr Aronson used to take our honours classes, and he stayed on for three years at Shantiniketan after Gurudev's death. He was born in Germany but fled to France after the rise of Hitler. There, he studied French and comparative literature before going to Cambridge University. He was in Shantiniketan from 1937 to 1944.

Since he was a German Jew, the last three years he spent in the Ashram, which spanned the Second World War, were full of tension. Often, we heard that a police party from Calcutta had come to his house and conducted raids, but never once did he let this stand in the way of his classes. He was always impeccably dressed in a khaddar pyjama and kurta and his lectures on Shakespeare are still a delightful memory. His amiable blue eyes that twinkled could become cold when his temper was roused, and his sharp look at any mischievous student was such a strong, silent reprimand that no one dared to play any tricks.

Dr Aronson and Marjorie Sykes were more Indian than most of us. Aron da always wore a loose khadi kurta pyjama, and occasionally even sported a tika of sandalwood paste on his forehead. A mild-mannered man, he rarely lost his temper except once when a student threw a non-poisonous snake into the classroom to frighten us. I still remember the day: Aron da was taking an English honours class and was deep into Shakespeare's *Twelfth Night*. 'If music be the food of love . . .' he read, when suddenly Boman Ghosh let loose that wretched reptile. As expected, the whole class screamed and Aron da leapt up, the book slipping away from his hand as he dodged the slithering snake. His face went red and he immediately caught hold of the culprit. He shook the pint-sized Boman by his collar, 'You rascal, you midget,' he roared in anger and then left the class without saying another word. We learnt later that snakes terrified him and that the incident had really shaken him.

A few years ago, when I had gone to Germany to participate in a Tagore seminar, I met Martin Kampchen, a scholar who lives in Shantiniketan and is studying various religions. He presented me his book, *Rabindranath Tagore and Germany*, which has a generous reference to Dr Aronson in the preface. I was reminded of the last time I met Dr Aronson, on the day he was leaving Shantiniketan and bidding us all goodbye. He has written somewhere, 'My students gave me a set of Tagore's books when I was leaving Shantiniketan, so I decided to quote some lines from his *Geetanjali* to them:

> When I go from hence
> Let this be my parting word
> That what I have seen
> Is unsurpassable . . .'

~

The other foreign teacher was Miss Marjorie Sykes: a tall, imposing figure, whose long legs and huge strides covered the Ashram from one end to the other in no time. She was soft-spoken, but that gentle speech was a contrast to her strict discipline in class. She preferred to make us slog in class rather than give us assignments to do at home so that she could ensure that no one had helped us write the essay. Arvind Mukherjee, whose older brother was the famous writer known all over Bengal as Banaphool, was a devil but he sat like a lamb in her class. Once, when all of us were bent over an essay she had set, and she was walking among us to keep an eye, Arvind waited for her to turn her back to his row and made an imaginary arrow to pierce her back. Some of us found it hard to suppress our giggles but perhaps God had given her eyes at the back of her head because Miss Sykes came down to where he was, her eyes sparkling with anger. Poor Arvind couldn't match her fiery gaze and lowered his eyes, then leapt to his feet and clasped her feet in both his hands, 'He Ma, Jagatdhatri, kshama koro, aar korbo na, korbo na! [O Mother Durga, forgive me! I'll never do it again!]'

His dramatic appeal and gesture were so funny that even the stern Miss Sykes broke into a smile.

Miss Sykes used to stay in a new bungalow in Kopai with a Santhal maid who wore a simple khadi sari, no blouse, and always had a bright red hibiscus flower stuck in her neat shiny bun. Her bare back, shining like a cobra's skin, was always uncovered. Above all, she had a hundred watt smile while flashing her white teeth at us. Till late into the night, Miss Sykes would sit at her desk and the maid would sit like a cat near her feet. She also had a strong, sweet voice and we learnt many Santhal folk songs from her. One that she was particularly fond of was:

Raja gelo shoroke-shoroke
Rani gelo kancha shoroke
Rajar chhata pare gelo jale
Rani hanslo mone-mone

[The raja was walking on the road
and his rani was walking on the mud path alongside.
The raja's umbrella fell into a puddle,
and the rani smiled quietly to herself]

Once in a while, Miss Sykes would summon one of us to take dictation. She was often unwell, and a bad cough made her breathless. So she would dictate to us while lying in her bed. The minute her maid saw one of us coming, her bored face would light up.

'Welcome, welcome, Didi! And what shall I get for you?'

'Doesn't your mistress scold you, Chandmani?'

She'd look at us in surprise, 'Why, Didi? Ma is like the Goddess Laxmi!'

~

Three of our gurus were renowned for their temper: Tanyendranath Ghosh, who taught us English in school; Professor Adhikari, who taught Indian philosophy; and Moshai, our geography teacher. Tanyendranath Ghosh's only daughter, Nandita (Baby di), was married to Nandalal Bose's son, Vishu da. Nandita di was a gifted dancer and we wondered how she tolerated her strict father's impossible rules. Perhaps he was gentler with his motherless daughter than he was with his students. We lived in terror of his classes. Yet it must be said that it was his strict adherence to rules that made us all fluent in English. 'Cross your t's and dot your i's,' he was fond of reminding us, else he would run a line through the entire assignment and throw the papers back at the hapless student. 'Remember that unless you give me a neatly written assignment, I will not even read it. I don't appreciate those who write their essays like doctors' prescriptions, understand?' I don't ever recall him laughing, and if he smiled, it was actually a smirk. 'He's smiling today,' we'd say. 'God knows whose turn it is today to get a whiplash.'

Once when I was unable to transcribe Chaucer's English correctly, he drew a cross on my face and made me stand under the maulsari tree for an hour. Today, I remember him with gratitude as I understand the necessity of discipline in life.

Professor Adhikari was a colleague of my scholar grandfather, Pandit Hariram Pande, in Banaras, and was among his closest friends. It was he who persuaded our grandfather to send the three of us siblings to faraway Shantiniketan, and for that I shall always be eternally grateful. One of his daughters, later known as Lady Ranu Mukherjee, was a renowned figure in Calcutta, and his other daughter was Asha (later Asha Aranyakam). Both the girls were escorted by my grandfather to the Ashram when they first came there from Banaras and so impressed was he by what he saw that he readily agreed to his friend's suggestion that he should send us here as well.

By the time Professor Adhikari came to the Ashram from Banaras, I was in BA, and he taught us Indian philosophy. A slight frame with a shining face and domed forehead, he sported a long white beard. He could not stand any chatter in his class and warned us at the beginning of his course, 'This is a deep and difficult subject. If you cannot hold your chatter and do not listen intently, don't bother to attend my classes.'

We never dared to transgress this rule until one day a snake charmer arrived with his *been* and *dafli* on the road that ran through the Ashram. Professor Adhikari always held his classes in the library, and the snake charmer's music wafted over through an open window. We all looked towards the maker of the music, but unfortunately Professor Adhikari's eyes only saw my face.

'Please leave the class this instant! Go! Follow that man to listen to his music to your heart's content,' he rapped.

I was paralysed.

'Didn't you hear me?' he said. 'Get out!'

I was in college by then and this humiliation in front of my fellow students really cut me. I got up quietly and sat on the steps outside the library. Then the bell rang, the class dispersed and in front of me stood Professor Adhikari.

'I am sorry, sir,' I mumbled, 'but I wasn't the only one . . .' and some tears fell on my cheeks.

'I know you weren't the only one,' he replied, 'but you are my friend's granddaughter and I have a right over you. I was giving you a talk on Mimansa and your attention was on that snake charmer's been. No one can understand Mimansa with that mesmerizing music in their ears and this is why I turned you out. I am sure that you will never allow yourself to be distracted from a lesson again.'

And he clip-clopped away on his wooden clogs.

I wonder if there is any teacher today who would dare to say, 'Get out!' to a student in a class of undergraduates.

~

Another guru whose cottage I considered a home away from home was Acharya Kshiti Mohan Sen. He always wore a khadi dhoti and his fair chest was covered by a Bhagalpuri *chadar*. His radiant face framed by his curly hair and white beard is clear in my mind's eye even after all these years. His granddaughter, Sunipa, was my friend, and their home, a part of Gurupalli, was surrounded by the homes of the other gurus of our Ashram. All of them had the same modest furniture and a courtyard at the back. The floor was covered by reed mats, books were strewn all over the room, and Acharya Sen would often place a portable half-desk on the takhat, which became a bed at night, to write. God knows how often we descended like locusts on this peaceful retreat to eat whatever was on offer. The memory of the delicious ber pickle (kuler achar) makes my mouth water. Some home-made sweets were always available, and often, if we were lucky, there was fried fish too. If his pretty daughters came home from Lucknow or Burma, we'd make it a point to arrive soon after them to savour the delicacies made for them. I often think of one of them, Amita di, and wonder if she would remember me with as much affection. Her little son, whom we all called Babloo, is now the renowned economist Amartya Sen. I remember how he would often visit our hostel and all of us would coo over him. Today, I find it difficult to imagine that this famous public intellectual once sat on my lap. How time flies!

As usual, I can do no better than quote some lines from Tagore:

Dinguli mor shonar khanchai
Rai lo na, rai lo na
Sheyi je amar nana ronger dinguli

[Alas, those golden days
have gone,
those colours have faded]

I had a selfish reason to visit Acharya Sen's house as well. Whenever there was a literary meet looming where I had to sing a bhajan, some of us would run to him for help. Invariably, he would provide us with a beautiful Meera or Kabir composition that was unsurpassable, and when someone as talented as Indulekha Ghosh would sing it, in Raga Poorvi, the effect was mesmerizing.

Acharya Sen often conducted the special prayer meeting held each Wednesday, and his deep baritone would convert the assembly hall into a temple. I close my eyes and can see him, his fair face with its sandalwood tilak, his folded hands as he sang, '*Andhakar theke amader alote niye jao, tomar je dokhin mukh* . . .'

I can also see the light filtering in from the stained glass windows playing a colourful game on his shining back while he was lost in prayer. He seemed then, and even now, the very epitome of divinity.

When I visited the same prayer hall after forty-five years, everything—including the stained-glass windows—was the same. Only our priest was absent. Time, like some cruel marauder, had taken away the precious idol that lay within that assembly hall.

~

Gurudev was very fond of outdoor celebrations. A full moon, especially in spring, when the Ashram was awash with a silvery light, was like a personal invitation from Mother Nature to us Ashramites. A notice would come round that we should all assemble at a particular spot in the Ashram that night. And lo and behold, all of us would bolt down an early dinner and head there to see what new treat awaited us. Among the assembly would be our maid, Khudu, and the kitchen boy, Nagendra, his dark, lithe body almost gleaming in that light. All the students—whether they were in Kala Bhavan, Shiksha Bhavan or Sangeet Bhavan—would saunter in one by one and you could say we resembled a marriage procession coming together. Someone would start a lovely song ('*Phaguner Purnima/Elo kar lipi haathe* . . . [Who has this Spring moon come to invite?]'). Singing lustily, we'd make a lazy circle of the Ashram and head towards Uttarayan, where Gurudev would be waiting for us. What better way to greet our Guru than sing him his own composition?

The audience would invariably have the Ashram's most devoted culture-vulture: our dear Sarju Maharaj. I must digress here to remember this extraordinary connoisseur of the arts. The Ashram had students from all corners of India and some were often homesick for food from their own region. This is why the Ashram started to employ cooks brought along by some of the students. For instance, Lakshmi Kanthamma Reddy, from Nellore in Andhra Pradesh, had brought their family retainer, Chellum, who made mouth-watering idlis, dosas, rasam-sambar, upma and other such delicacies. Naturally, this started an avalanche of other culinary experts: we now had a Gujarati cook, a Sinhalese cook, and even a Chinese cook. Only us poor students from north India had no one to cook us our favourite food, because no cook from Uttar Pradesh would agree to come so far away from home. This is how Sarju Maharaj, from Chhapra in Bihar, arrived to take care of us and dish out the arhar dal and baigan ka bharta that we longed to eat. However, it soon became evident that his heart lay elsewhere—he was a musician and since even the leaves of the Ashram were steeped in music, he felt that he was in the best workplace God had created. There were rehearsals almost every day somewhere in the Ashram. The minute Sarju Maharaj got wind of any rehearsal, he would quickly finish cooking (often dinner was ready by five in the evening!) and take off. He knew the words of every song composed by Gurudev but gave them his own unique touch by adding 'He Rama' at certain intervals he deemed fit. Thus, one of Gurudev's most famous *Varshamangal* songs ('*Pagla hawa, badal dine, pagal amaar man jeyge uthe*') became something else after that special Sarju Maharaj touch.

'*Pagla hawa, He Rama, Badal dine pagal amaar man jeyge uthe, He Rama . . .*' he sang lustily.

Sarju came religiously to every rehearsal, his head covered with his signature red *gamchha*, ready to sing along.

Whether it was *Chitrangada*, *Chandalika*, *Mayar Khela* or *Tasher Desh*, Gurudev would personally direct their rehearsals. The polished red floor of the stage would reverberate with the tinkle of ankle bells as the dancers glided across it. Guru Kelu Nambiar would be instructed by Gurudev on the expressive context of the song to inspire him to choreograph a suitable piece. Those of us who have seen his choreography of '*jol daao, more jal daao* . . . [Water! Give me a drink of water . . .]' with Tagore's granddaughter, Nandita Kriplani, perfectly enacting the whole sequence of drawing water out of a well and pouring it into the cupped hands of the thirsty traveller, will never forget it. Nandita di, whom we all knew by her pet name, Burhi di, was a special friend. I can still see before my eyes her face as it was then: fair, with large eyes and a lovely gurgle of laughter. She stayed with her grandfather in the 'Thakurbadi' and took part in virtually every dance drama that Gurudev composed. I once accompanied her and Gurudev to Almora and stayed a few days in the huge Tagore mansion, 'Jorasanko'. When I saw them together, I realized how Tagore doted on this special granddaughter.

Let me briefly recount that memorable trip to Almora with Gurudev, preparations for which were no less complex than the viceroy's annual transfer of capital. Accompanying Gurudev was Burhi di's mother, Meera di, and his secretary, Annada Babu. Till late in the night, Burhi di packed his woollen gowns, books, paints, brushes and all the other paraphernalia that a writer and artist would need in the hills. Meanwhile, she also took me on a conducted tour of that huge palace. I still remember those spiral cast-iron staircases and endless rooms. Then, we sat in the long veranda and she sang a beautiful song for me. That song was inspired by the *pahari* folk tune Gurudev had once heard in Ramgarh and been haunted by:

Door deshi sheyi
Rakhal chhele . . .

I see her lovely face as clearly now as all those years ago: her carelessly tied sari, one end thrown over a shoulder in the Bengali style, and long gold earrings swinging as she sang on. Who could have ever guessed that that lovely young face would be ravaged one day by cancer? Her husband, Krishna Kripalani, was the secretary of the Sahitya Akademi in Delhi, and they had moved out of their lovely home in Calcutta, where we had spent many fun-filled evenings. I happened to be in Delhi when I heard that Burhi di was battling cancer, but when I went to see her at the hospital, I had to return disappointed. They would not allow visitors to see patients outside of visiting hours, and no matter how hard I pleaded, they refused to relax that rule. I came away recalling Gurudev's immortal lines:

> Dware eshe gaile phire
> Parshane dwar jete khue . . .
>
> [You went away after coming to my door.
> Had you but touched it, my door would have let you
> in . . .]

I wrote her a letter when I reached Nainital and she immediately answered it:

> I was so upset to hear that you were not allowed in even
> though you had come from so far to see me that day.
> You have mentioned that you are writing a book on
> our Ashram. Don't forget to send me a copy when you
> publish it.

I have completed the book, Burhi di, but even if I want to, I cannot send it to the address where you have gone now.

Nandita di, Mamata Bhattacharya, Hansu, Anita Baruah, Vanleela Bhatt, Stree—these dancers were groomed personally by Gurudev. Once when Gurudev was being honoured by some society in Cuttack, a thin, emaciated girl sang a song composed in honour of his visit. So struck was he by her voice that he immediately wanted to know who she was. He was told that she belonged to a poor family. They found it hard to even provide a bellyful of food to their children, so where was the money for music lessons? Gurudev promised that he would nurture her talent and called her to his Ashram, where she was admitted to Sangeet Bhavan. Another indigent student, Kalu, was blind but what a voice he had! Gurudev took him in as well.

Every other week, students would organize a literary evening, and everyone wanted Gurudev to preside over it. So it was decided that every bhavan (school) would be given time for a literary evening each month. If he was unable to attend it personally, he would send across a bouquet of roses from his garden and promise to make it up the next time.

~

On Gandhiji's birth anniversary, the Ashram devised a special way to pay its tribute to him. All the staff would be given the day off, and the teachers and students would take over their work for that day. The previous day, a list was pasted on our notice board to inform every member about what they were expected to do. Some were assigned kitchen work, others had to take over the sweeping and swabbing, still others were given the toilets and bathrooms to scrub. What a joy it was to peel mounds of potatoes or weep over onions! I laugh now when I remember our happiness at these miserable tasks. But the next day, bandaged fingers or limping legs would tell their own tales of how that fun ended! In the evening, special games, such as kabaddi and kho-kho, were organized for the staff.

2 October always began with a special prayer meeting in Amrakunj. I recall one year when Gurudev himself addressed us. 'Today, as we celebrate Gandhiji's birthday, we Ashramites must undertake a pledge. I have always wanted to catch the first stirrings of human hope, so let us ask ourselves, where do we place the man whose birth we celebrate on this day? What is that special quality that distinguishes him? I think it lies in his firm resolve that has bound together this whole country. The awareness he has generated is electric, it is unprecedented. It is as if Gandhiji has managed to prise loose a huge boulder that had been placed on our chests to pin us in eternal servitude.'

Each time Gandhiji went on a hunger strike, the Ashram was plunged into gloom and worry. On one such occasion, Gurudev had summoned us all to declare: 'I salute the *tapasvi* who faces death with such calm. Place God in your hearts and light your hearts with the flame of love. Your hosannas of praise for Gandhiji should be so loud that they reach him with all our love and pride. Let him know that we are all behind him on the path of truth that he has shown us. Remember that Gandhiji's message is not heard by the ears alone: it pierces our hearts. Alas, my language does not have that magical quality! But the language Gandhiji speaks is the universal voice of man; it resides in each of our hearts. I am sure you can all hear it.' As he neared the end of this sentence, Gurudev's voice began to tremble.

When Gandhiji arrived at the Ashram in February 1940, a virtual flood of celebrations was organized. The universal language that Gurudev had mentioned once had reached our hearts and set them singing. So, when, in 1942, a young martyr gave up his life for Gandhiji's cause, we were all convinced that his heart had been pierced by Gandhiji's message as well. I have never seen a mention of this act of patriotism anywhere, but we all thought that this little martyr was no less brave than Khudi Ram, Bhagat Singh or Azad. Let me remember him.

Dhruv Kundu, a happy ten- or twelve-year-old boy, was a student of the Ashram's nursery section, Shishu Bhavan. He wore a khaddar kurta and half-pants and had a head full of tight, curly black hair. Dhruv came from Purnea in Bihar and that was why his Bangla was tinged with a lovely sing-song Bihari lilt. His father, Dr Kundu, was a member of the Congress Party who often came to visit his daughter, Shantilata, an inmate of the girls' hostel. Dr Kundu was a widower and he doted on his little son. After his father returned to Purnea, little Dhruv would come running to our hostel, waving the five-rupee note his father always handed to him at the end of each visit to his children. 'Know what this is, Didi?' he'd ask me. 'Baba gave it to me!'

Shanti was my friend and since she called me 'didi', I became Dhruv's didi as well. He'd snuggle up to me and list the many things he planned to buy with that note—cashew nuts, lozenges and toffees. 'Do you want chanachur, Didi?' he'd ask me. 'I'll get some for you,' he added generously. I still remember his bright eyes, which sparkled like glass marbles in his happy face. He'd hang around our hostel for hours, chattering with all the other didis until his own arrived and threw him out, saying: 'Why are you still here? Are you planning to spend the night or something? Go, run! It is almost time for the evening prayers.' He'd flash a last, lingering look at all of us and get up reluctantly.

One day, he arrived with a tear-blotched face and asked me, 'Is Didi around?'

'Why? What happened?' I asked him and he stuck out his knee. He'd had a fight with another boy and grazed his knee in the scuffle. 'I'll ask Didi to fix him,' he declared and started sobbing again. Shanti heard his voice and came running. The knee was not badly hurt but his heart was. 'I promise, Didi,' he sobbed, 'I did nothing. He snatched away my marbles . . .'

'Aha, my little Ganesh,' his sister replied. 'All you know is how to eat the laddoos, don't you? Can't you fight your own battles?'

Poor Dhruv, who hardly knew how to even raise his voice in anger, was not the type who would punch a bully. Shanti and I bathed his knee, wiped his face and combed his hair. 'Go now, it's getting dark.' Shanti said. 'Now remember, the next time this happens, don't come here crying like a baby. Understand?'

'Walk with me up to the kitchen, Didi,' he begged. 'I'm scared.'

'What are you scared of, you silly boy?' Shanti laughed back.

'The devil and witches that lurk in the dark,' he replied.

'Come on, Dhruv,' I added. 'You are a little man, go with your chest stuck out—they'll run away. What are you afraid of?'

Little Dhruv puffed out his chest as I had suggested and went forth to confront the devil and any lurking witches like a man. Sometime later, when I was leaving for Almora at the end of our exams, he came running one evening, stuffed a clumsy packet in my hands and ran away. I opened it to find a clay parrot he had made in his craft class and laughed at this token of love. If only I had known then what was to happen, I would have preserved that little parrot for the rest of my life and covered its beak with gold.

After the vacations, we were all told of the sad news from Purnea. Little Dhruv Kundu, proudly holding aloft a tricolour flag, was part of a protest march. In the police firing that followed, a stray bullet hit him and he died a martyr. I was stunned by the news, unable to believe that little Dhruv, who clung to my hand as soon as he heard a footfall in the dark, was dead. How could I have told him to be fearless; he was a man, I'd told him. He couldn't afford to be afraid!

In his death, he proved to all of us that he indeed was the only man among us all.

~

Among the several festivals we celebrated in the Ashram, the seventh day of Paush was my favourite. We'd rise at dawn and head towards Shriniketan, sharing the carts with the huge cooking vessels that were used to cook our lunch there. The Ashram's cooks, musical like all its inmates, had concocted a song to remind us to be ready at four in the morning if we wanted a lift.

I remember it ran like this:

Babuji, Baabuji
Shokale charta baje
Panchta kaino bajena
Babuji, Baabuji . . .

[Babuji,
four o'clock in the morning is too early
Why not five in the evening,
Babuji . . .]

The *kutcha* path to Shriniketan was strewn with nettles and bushes, and somewhere on the way was a cremation ground. Marked off by a small wall, the deserted grounds were strewn with smashed terracotta pots, bits of rope and a few bamboo poles, unhappy remnants of past cremations. Some would irreverently giggle as they chanted 'Bol Hari, Hari bol,' the chant that accompanied the bier to the cremation grounds with the pallbearers. Immediately, Sarojini di would reprimand them, 'Aren't you ashamed of your behaviour? This is where a man ends his life! Say Durga, Durga instead!' Suitably chastened, we'd all start chanting 'Durga, Durga' as instructed.

Sarojini di's faith in Durga was legendary. If, at night, strange sounds came from the dark forest surrounding the Ashram, her remedy to banish fright was, 'Chant Dugga, Dugga.' She'd close her eyes and touch her forehead with folded hands while she muttered a silent prayer to her favourite Goddess. 'These are *takshaks*,' she'd tell us solemnly, 'a kind of evil goblin.'

We'd wind our way along the bumpy path covered with red gravel and shout with joy as we spotted the 'Bada Shahaber Kuti' (the Big Sahib's house). This was a three-storey mansion, studded with gleaming glass windows, large, airy rooms, grand spiral staircases—quite unlike anything we had in Shantiniketan. It was said that it once belonged to some rich indigo plantation owner. Later, the Ashram bought it.

We would tumble out of the bullock carts and run to occupy the spaces within. Songs rang out from every room, some played cards, someone ran to buy oily pakodas from a small shop outside, and the fun would start.

~

What we received in the Ashram was not mere lifeless education. In 1912, Gurudev wrote: 'Where education is concerned, I made an important discovery. Man alone can teach man exactly as water feeds an ocean, fire lights a lamp and life nurtures life . . .'

I remain awed at the memory of the teachers we had: Pearson, Professor Ta'an, Vidhushekhar Bhattacharya, Nitai Vinod Goswami, Hajari Prasad Dwivedi, Marjorie Sykes, Alex Aronson, Kshiti Mohan Sen, Nandalal Basu, Maulana Alimuddin, and Gurudev himself. So how does one even begin to convey what Tagore meant to all the children who passed through his Ashram? He has written somewhere: 'Jeewanta shudhu pathe chale nahe . . . [Life is not about walking along a set path . . .]'

Years ago, Professor Ta'an's three-year-old son, Ta'an Li, read out three lines that he had composed in honour of

Gurudev. The tiny tot, dressed in a spotless white kurta and dhoti, won everyone's hearts with his sweet round face and neat hair. I was present and can still hear his sweet prattle because those lines are etched in my heart:

> *Guludev boro bhalo*
> *Amla jonke bhalo bashi*
> *Guludev amar ma*
>
> [Guludev is very nice,
> he loves us all very much.
> Guludev is our mother]

I don't think any poet or admirer of Tagore has captured his personality more vividly than little Ta'an Li.

A Dark Cloud Descends
on the Ashram

By the end of my stay there, Shantiniketan had become famous all over the country and beyond. Scores of students from foreign countries arrived to see and learn from the extraordinary Ashram Gurudev had created and nurtured. However, between the joy of learning new ways and the celebration of festivals the Tagore way, it had become evident to several inmates that the rays of the sun that we all revolved around had begun to dim.

Outwardly, however, the Ashram carried on as usual. In fact, a new power house was being built exclusively for our Ashram, and Gurudev had pointed to it, saying, 'After this is completed, you will never face any problems with electricity in your rooms.' Yet, it had become apparent to us that the power supply to our inner dynamos that charged us with such energy was slowly running out of time. The question uppermost in all our minds was what or who could ever replace the real centre of power of our Ashram?

Gurudev was ageing and his health had begun to show signs of an ominous decline. We would still go singing his songs to his home, Uttarayan, but no longer could we bring to those songs the full-throated joy of our earlier enthusiastic offerings. Our festivals and celebrations no longer had the spontaneity and joy that once gave them their true energy. We all watched from afar as several eminent doctors arrived from Calcutta to examine him and noted their grim expressions when they departed.

The face that had appeared to be lit up with some divine light, and the glow that I had first seen that evening long ago when I first met Gurudev, was fading. All of us would huddle together anxiously each evening to share our collective concern: a fearful foreboding of a tragedy about to strike our lives. Gurudev's long locks had been trimmed and his frame seemed to shrink before our eyes with each passing week.

Then came the news that he was being shifted to Calcutta for treatment. Every evening, crowds of us would stand outside Uttarayan in a silent vigil, praying for him and ourselves. During the day, so many teachers—several among them his students—would snap their books shut and dismiss the class, unable to carry on as usual. In the prayer hall, Upasana Bhavan, Kshiti Mohan Babu would inexplicably fall silent as he led the prayers for Gurudev's health by singing one of the famed Tagore hymns. It was as if a dark cloud had descended on the Ashram and dimmed the light over it.

And then, inevitably, Tagore was shifted to Calcutta. The whole Ashram turned out to say goodbye, aware that this may be the last time we would see him alive. One by one, we touched his feet and carried the dust to our foreheads. Not a word was spoken and none was needed. As the Ashram's bus drove away carrying its precious passenger, we followed it as far as we could with moist eyes and then lost him in a cloud of departing dust.

All-night vigils and prayer cycles became our way of sending him our love. A huge blackboard, set up outside the library, supplied us with the daily health bulletin received from Calcutta, and its message was: 'Gurudev's condition remains critical.' Ultimately, we were told about his demise and it seemed as if a royal crown had been robbed of its most precious jewel.

Gurudev's ashes were brought back by his family to the Ashram and all the inmates lined up on both sides to receive them, heads bent and hearts heavy with grief.

Among the prayers that were sung at the Ashram was one he had once composed:

Aamaar jaabar shomoy holo,
amay keno rakhish dhore?
Chokher joler bandhon diye
bandhish ne aar mayadore.
Phuriyechhe jiboner chhuti,
phiriye ne tor noyon duti.
Naam dhore aar dakish ne bhai,
jete hobe twora kore . . .

[It is time for me to go,
so why are you holding me back?
Release me from the loving tears that bind you to me.
The play of life is over,

turn your eyes away
Don't look at me,
or call me by my name.
Set me free . . .]

Even after so many decades, I can see him as clearly as when I saw him for the first time: bent over a desk, his noble head topped with his signature headgear, so absorbed in his writing that he gives a little start when he hears our footsteps. He raises his head to say, '*Ki re . . . abaar ki haulo*? [What's happened now, girl?]'

Then I hear him recite another poem:

Shomukhe shanti paaraabaar
Bhashao toruni he karnodhar

[An ocean of peace lies before me
Oarsman, let my boat sail on its bosom]

PART II

Friends and Others

That Little Drop of Dew!

The first round of a seminar on Tagore had just ended in Dumstadt's vast hall when someone came up to me to announce: 'The German radio has just flashed the news that Satyajit Ray is no more.' I had never called Satyajit Ray by his real name; to us Ashramites, he was always Manik da, although none of us knew then that one day he would shine as brightly as the ruby of that affectionate nickname.

I turned my face towards the windows to hide my tears. Grey rain clouds rolled outside, almost as if someone was drawing black drapes before arranging a condolence meeting in heaven. As I watched the trembling leaves, shivering in the rain outside the windows, a deep sadness seeped over me. And yet, I wasn't alone in my grief—the entire assembly lapsed into a hushed silence as the news spread. Here I was, miles away from my homeland, I thought, mourning my friend along with hundreds of people I did not even know by name.

A host of memories crowded my mind and I shook my head to clear the pictures. We had all known for some time now that Manik da was living on borrowed time. His enfeebled heart was battling valiantly to keep that splendid frame alive but we knew it was just a matter of time before Yama, the God of Death, would swoop in triumphantly and take him away from us. They say that Yama is totally without compassion when he comes down to claim his prize. And yet, recently, when I heard Manik da's familiar baritone accepting the Lifetime Achievement Award from the American Academy of Motion Pictures, I thought to myself that no one with a booming voice like that could be so seriously ill! Who knows, this time too he would recover as he did when he returned from the US after Dr Denton Cooley had dragged him back from the brink of death, I had thought. After all, he had come back then and completed an unfinished film.

He was still recovering from that bout of illness when I last met him in Calcutta. Four years before that last meeting, when I had come to Calcutta, Manik da had come to meet me. My daughter's father-in-law, B.D. Pande, was then the West Bengal governor, and he had thoughtfully arranged for all my Ashram friends to come to the Raj Bhavan one evening. We fell upon each other's necks in joy. Manik da, Suchitra Mitra, my dearest school friend Anima Sen, the daughter-in-law of our respected teacher, Acharya Kshiti Mohan Sen, Arundhati Mukherji, Tara Sarkar . . .

'Ours must have surely been the Golden Age of Shantiniketan,' I had declared loftily as I looked proudly at that assembly of famous personages that day.

'Don't ever forget,' Manik da reminded us solemnly, 'that whatever we are today is because of what we learnt at the Ashram.' He always spoke in measured, reflective tones and

I suddenly felt as chastened as a schoolgirl rapped on her knuckles for overlooking a basic fact.

The Calcutta I once knew had changed so irrevocably since I was a student that I had to ask one Dr Upadhyaya from the university to accompany me, unsure that I would be able to trace Satyajit Ray's house on my own. Dr Upadhyaya was ecstatic at the prospect of meeting Calcutta's living legend and he kept thanking me for taking him along. We rang the bell outside that famous flat on Bishop Lefroy Road and Manik da opened the door himself. The veranda was full of potted plants that he had probably been spraying with water when we arrived. I had planned this visit on a sudden impulse, without even a formal appointment, yet I found myself being greeted warmly when I reached. 'What a pleasant surprise,' Manik da smiled at me as he led us in. I could see several people (probably with appointments made long ago) waiting to meet him as Manik da took us into his den. A huge portrait of his father, Sukumar Ray, dominated one wall of an otherwise spartan, cell-like room, strewn with papers.

Manik da was a giant of a man, and his tall frame remained ever erect and slim. His voice, like the deep boom of a temple bell, drew attention whenever he spoke. But that day, for the first time, I felt he had aged. His face had changed so much in the last four years that he now looked terribly gaunt and tired. And his voice no longer boomed, perhaps because he had a sore throat that day. Yet, when he smiled at me, or threw back his head to laugh in a particular way, he became once more the Manik da I had always known and admired.

Manik da was never a talker; in fact, he gave the impression of weighing every word he uttered and that is what probably gave his speech its air of deep, reflective gravity. I jabbered on and he listened attentively as usual until I became aware that the crowd of admirers waiting outside kept growing. Embarrassed at having taken up so much of his time, I got up to leave. 'Sit, sit,' he kept saying but I excused myself. I could kick myself today for leaving that room so soon but I had no idea then that this would be our last meeting.

'All right, at least have a rasagulla before you leave,' he smiled. 'I know you love them. I've seen you eating them at Kalu's shop in the Ashram,' he added wickedly.

My jaw dropped at this piece of news. We used to be in such awe of him then that the fact that he had even noticed my love of rasagullas was a revelation. In our Ashram days, Manik da would stride past a gaggle of us without lifting his eyes. Kalu's shop was our favourite haunt; the rasagullas were so spongy that you had to squeeze the syrup out before popping one in your mouth, else you could choke.

Manik da was a great friend of my elder brother, Tribhuvan, and I think somewhere in his mind I was always a sort of pesky younger sister. Occasionally, I gathered the courage to talk to him but for the rest we left him and his gang well alone. In those days, apart from his aloof air, he was famous in the Ashram as the son of the legendary Sukumar Ray. Often, his mother—an elegant and dignified lady— would come and stay at Uttarayan, Tagore's home. She was an expert needlewoman and I remember once being given lessons in *kantha* embroidery by her. Unfortunately, I never got to know Manik da's wife but I was great friends with her elder sister, Gauri di. Whenever Gauri di came to Bombay, she would stay with Sushila—another Ashramite friend—and call me. 'Hurry up and come over,' she'd order. 'I've made some payesh with new gur today.'

Gauri di was Kishore Kumar's mother-in-law and Amit Kumar's grandmother. As she watched us lick the payesh bowls clean, she would sigh and say, 'If only Amit had been able to come as well. He loves my payesh!'

I had asked her about Manik da last the last time we met in Bombay. Her smiling face clouded over: 'What can I say?' she shook her head sadly. 'He is a shell of his former self now. It frightens me to see how frail he is getting.'

Several times, I lifted my pen to write about him and then put it down again. With the hundreds of important letters that must have poured into his Calcutta house, what worth would mine have? Better to go back to our days in the Ashram and remember him as he was then. Once, when we staged the play *Sinha Sadan*, I was given the part of a Muslim boy. A fez cap was procured from Bolpur and someone suggested I borrow a pair of churidar pyjamas and a kurta from Jayant Desai, a student of Kala Bhavan.

I paled. Jayant was a renowned misogynist and asking him for anything meant getting your head bitten off. Anyway, I went. He looked me up and down and then asked: 'Are you Tribhuvan's sister?'

I nodded.

'All right, take this.' He stiffly held out a pair of churidars and a kurta. 'Don't you dare cut it up! And wash it before you bring it back,' he added, as if I had some unspeakable disease.

Jayant Desai was at least three times my size; no matter how hard I tried to tuck in the kurta, it just would not fit. As for his churidars! Even if I had tied them around my neck, I doubt I would have managed to get into them. Thankfully, another friend, Jitendra Pratap, who was about as tall as I was, lent me his sherwani to tuck the kurta into. I remember he took a photograph of me that day—perhaps he still has it somewhere.

Our make-up artist was Gauri di, Nandalal Bose's daughter, and she gave me such a splendid makeover that day that even my mother would have failed to recognize me. The master stroke was a moustache that she cunningly painted over my lips. She saw her handiwork and dissolved into helpless giggles: 'You look like an absolute goonda now!' she declared. When the rest of my gang saw me they hooted with laughter. One of them, Sandhya Roy, flung her arms around my neck and whispered, 'If you were truly a boy, I would be your lover!' Another one, Jaya Appasamy, looked at me critically and said, 'You know, if you were to smoke a cigarette, you would look perfect.'

Fifty years ago, a girl who smoked was a rare sight and in the Ashram, one would not even dream of lighting up. If someone sent a letter to my grandfather in Almora, I told Jaya di, I'd be thrown out of the family for sure.

'I'm not asking you to smoke a real cigarette, silly,' Jaya di replied. 'Just roll some ajwain seeds in a piece of paper and blow a few smoke rings. That's all!'

And that is exactly what I did. You should have heard the applause my performance got. So when, a few days later, a handwritten magazine taken out by some Ashramites reached my hands, my blood boiled with rage. 'Does it become a girl from the Ashram to smoke openly on the stage?' someone had written spitefully. 'We feel she should be suitably punished.'

There was no name at the bottom of the comment but we were sure that one of Manik da's buddies was behind this. I stormed up to him, waving the magazine angrily in front of me. 'Do you even know what I smoked?' I lashed out. 'It was just ajwain seeds. I can produce twenty witnesses who will swear to this. Why could you all not have said something about my great performance, tell me?'

I still blush with shame when I recall my furious tirade. Did I really have the temerity to ask the most famous director of all time to praise my performance that day? Manik da listened to my outpouring with no expression except a faint smile. Not once did he say to me, 'When I did not write that, why are you telling me this?' Many days later, his friend Soumendra came to me and apologized for having written that article. 'But why did you have to yell at Manik da?' he asked me. 'The poor chap knew I was the guilty one but kept quiet.'

On another occasion, we had all gone on a picnic. Every year, the Ashram would take us on a picnic to Shiyori or Kopai or Shriniketan for an outing. All the Shantiniketan students—whether they were from Kala Bhavan, Shiksha Bhavan, Sangeet Bhavan or Vidya Bhavan—joined in. Accompanying us were bullock carts loaded with huge pots and pans, firewood and provisions. Our meal was cooked in the open and all of us sat down together to eat delicious khichri, curd, fish and vegetable curry off leaf plates. At the end of the feast, Kshitij da, who oversaw the whole affair, would ask loudly, '*Laglo kaimon?* [How was it?]'

And all of us would roar together: '*Besh*! [Wonderful!]' and then, '*Guruji ki fateh*! [Long live the Guru!]'.

The cooks were our Ashram ones: Harihar, Nagendra, a south Indian cook called Chellum, one from Bihar called Sarju, and presiding over them was Sarojini di, whom Acharya Hajari Prasad Dwivedi had christened 'Annapurna'. That year, her son Rahul had suddenly died, leaving behind a young widow, Ranu Boudi. Even that could not keep her from coming. 'This picnic happens just once a year. If I don't go along, something may go wrong,' she had said.

Only those of us who were fortunate enough to have attended those picnics will know what they were like. There was our music teacher, Shailaj Majumdar, with his israj, and then there was Amita di, her lovely voice soaring over the plains:

O anather nath
O agatir gati . . .

She never needed a mike; her strong voice floated across to us on the breeze. Then Kanika di would sing that lovely song, '*Baje karun svare . . .*', that Gurudev had specially set in a Carnatic raga for a favourite student from the south, Savitri di. She would be followed by Kundamunda Reddy. His voice was like a thundercloud that rolls against the mountains. And then, Kshitij da would conduct a chorus:

Rangay . . .

The main voice would be that of our English teacher, Kshitij Ray, whose cheerful face was topped with a jaunty beret. A few years ago, when I ran into him at a function, my eyes filled up when I saw what old age had done to him. He had lost his lovely wife and then his beloved daughter. Now left alone, he was laid up with a broken leg. When I went to see him, he was propped up in an easy chair and a tiffin carrier was placed within easy reach.

He probably saw the horror on my face at this state of loneliness. 'A boy fetches me some food from the canteen,' he said wryly. 'And I lie here all day, remembering the chatter of your voices from the past.'

The other day, here in Germany, I met his daughter, Sharmila. She had been specially invited to sing for the seminar on Tagore where I was invited to speak as well. I did not know who she was, but because she was the spitting image of her mother, Uma di, I was able to place her at once. Married to a Frenchman, she now lives in France and has done a great deal to popularize Rabindra sangeet in Europe.

'Once in a while I go to visit Baba,' she started, 'but it isn't easy to travel to India frequently,' and then her eyes filled up with tears. Her Baba was once the life and soul of the Ashram's annual picnic, I tell her, and suddenly I am reminded of Manik da once again. Our old cook Harihar had got lost after a picnic to Rangamati that year. We all called out, but our voices came back to us like empty boomerangs. There was no sign of the old man and everyone started to panic. Then someone suggested we ask Manik da to call out Harihar's name. 'His voice can reach Burdwan,' the man had quipped.

Manik da, no doubt disgusted by our childish high jinks, had moved away from our noisy group and was sketching, his back propped up against a tree trunk. Who would bell the cat? Finally, we managed to persuade his friend Soumendra to carry our request to the Artist under the Tree. We could see the two arguing over something, then Manik da reluctantly got up and called in his deep baritone, 'Harihar, O Harihar . . .', and I think even the forest stopped to hear him.

A little later, a sheepish and frightened Harihar arrived, saying, 'Thank God you called, Babu, I was hopelessly lost!' Manik da's clarion call had worked. It was the same clarion call that was to rouse another lost soul later—the soul of Bengal's lost artistic heritage. He may have been best known for his films but there was hardly any artistic endeavour in Bengal that remained untouched by Ray's spectacular genius. In this respect, he was not unlike that other Renaissance man—his guru, Rabindranath Tagore. Manik da once wrote: 'Poetry, drama, the novel, painting, music, philosophy and education—in all these fields, Tagore's contribution is even greater than that of Shakespeare. I am a Bengali myself, and can say confidently that where music is concerned, few composers can match the genius of Tagore. And I include Western musicians as I say this. Not merely as a poet, even as a novelist, Tagore remains unique. His essays have an astonishing range and reflect his far-sighted vision, a quality not often encountered in other essayists. And his fiction characters bear a stamp of his incomparable genius.'

This is probably why Satyajit Ray used Tagore time and again in his films and often his music too.

Refrains from Rabindra sangeet, such as '*Ami chini go, chini tomaare, Ogo videshini . . .*' (*Charulata*) are subtly used. This song, based on Tagore's '*Enichchi mora enichchi mora*' (from

Valmiki Pratibha), followed a Western notational system. The other day, when Sharmila sang several of these Western melodies from Rabindra sangeet to present the cosmopolitan aspect of Tagore's musical genius, the German audience was utterly charmed.

The same cosmopolitan quality was reflected in Ray's work as well and this is what made him so popular outside India. His brilliant blending of time, situation, character and narrative into a musical universe was quite unique. And it was a gift that Ray always used to his advantage.

He writes: 'Film and music have a marvellous harmony. Both respect time, pace, metre and the human heart. Melancholy, joy, reflection—these moods have nourished Western music. Our own music heritage is entirely different. Indian classical music is less dramatic, more ornamental.'

Probably to take up Ray's challenge, two film-makers actually went to Paris to study Western classical music, but as Shyam Benegal has written somewhere, their intellectual arrogance could never dent the natural genius of Ray.

Ray reflected deeply on whatever he thought and did and managed to transform complex thought processes into a single visual image. I doubt if anyone has been able to, or can ever, equal that. He was like a river in spate—no canal or rivulet could hope to match the intensity of his artistic flow. From the early phase of his film-making that included the Apu trilogy, *Parash Pathar* and *Jalsaghar* to the later one of *Charulata, Ashani Sanket, Hirak Rajar Deshe, Sonar Kella* and *Aranyer Din Ratri* to the final clutch of *Shakha Proshakha* and *Ganashatru*, his genius remained as pristine and strong as always.

What Ray placed before us was a thrillingly new visual universe—our everyday world with a completely new dimension. To every spectator—whether he was from the Punjab, the far south or Maharashtra—Ray's films did not present characters that were tied to a narrow parochial world. His characters spoke to us all equally. Every gust of breeze, every patter of raindrops in his films touched us all with the same intensity. The men and women we saw in his films had faces that we knew and empathized with because their wrinkles were etched with our pain.

Ray's magic wand transformed his actors (from Soumitra Chatterjee in a host of his films to Madhabi Mukherji in *Charulata*, Sharmila Tagore in *Apur Sansar* and Aparna Sen in *Teen Kanya*) into characters that were greater than their reputations. All his actors acknowledged this and this is why, perhaps, Madhabi wrote in *Satyajit Ray at 70*[*] that in *Mahanagar*, 'Ray gave me a new life. He opened a tiny window for me that looked out into a huge world. I was just a lump of clay that he moulded first into a statue and then gave the gift of sight.'

Rajendra Yadav wrote recently that fiction has lost its heroes and heroines—just memories of them now remain. Memoirs, not fiction, are the future, he seems to imply.

It isn't that they have died—I want to tell him—they are still alive; it is just that we have forgotten how to recognize them when we see them. And even if we do, we turn our gaze away, for to recognize them would mean the defeat of our ability to create them. Our arrogance forbids us to even acknowledge their presence. Satyajit Ray knew this well,

---

[*] Nemai Ghosh, *Satyajit Ray at 70* (Delhi: Orient BlackSwan, 1993).

and his films never failed in identifying the real heroes and heroines of our times. He showed us the indomitable human spirit in all its frailties and weaknesses, but also recognized its strength and resilience. Nothing escaped Ray's eye, especially not the vulnerable spirit of man. His ability to present the human spirit before us was responsible for Ray's success as an artist of the camera.

As for memoirs, I believe that they nourish the world of fiction. That is, if our own arrogance does not creep in while recording them. Our lives change, values change, our likes and dislikes change too. How can we not reflect this in what we leave for the coming generations to feel and know?

After Manik da's death, somehow I could never get myself to write about him. The world had mourned him in so many ways—letters, seminars, memorial services—where did I stand in this line of admirers, I thought. I belonged to another world and felt as Sudama must have when he went to the court of Lord Krishna. I did not know Satyajit Ray as intimately as many others did. To me he always was and will continue to be Manik da—a gentle giant whose gaunt face lit up with a special smile when I rang his doorbell one day in Calcutta, and who remembered to get me a rasagulla, and who came to the door to see me off. How can I forget such a man?

India has always taken a long time to recognize its precious jewels; even Bhartrihari became a venerable figure to us when an English missionary translated his work and made it known to the world. Kalidasa was placed on a pedestal when German scholars recognized his genius, and Rabindranath Tagore became an icon after he was awarded the Nobel Prize. Maharishi Raman and Swami Vivekananda, too, came to us via the West, with the Western hallmark of excellence before we recognized their genius. What about Ramanujan, the mathematical prodigy who nearly starved to death here? I often wonder whether our anglicized reading public would ever have gone towards the Upanishads if T.S. Eliot had not been born. Ray, too, became a national treasure when his first film won accolades abroad.

~

My mother had a beautiful wooden chest, studded with brass nails, where she kept all her treasures. It had once belonged to our grandfather, and each time she opened it, we would crowd round it to inhale the delicate fragrance it exuded and listen to her stories. It was my mother's personal archive, and the delicate fragrance, I discovered later, came from a bag of musk, palm-leaf manuscripts and a tiger claw mounted on gold. One of the most precious objects there was the placenta of a cat, which—so my mother said—was more difficult to procure than anything in the world. 'If someone actually succeeds in tricking a cat to procure one,' my mother would tell us goggle-eyed children, 'then the Goddess of Wealth, Lakshmi, will never abandon your home.' She would show us her precious coral beads, taken from a courtesan's necklace because it was said that the woman who wore it would never be widowed. Over time, after she had shared it with many women, she had just a few beads left. A palm-leaf manuscript, with my grandmother's delicate handwriting, had lines from the Raghuvansh, Manas and Bhoj Prabandh. I think my daughter Mrinal has a few pieces of it.

Among my own treasures were a sketch of me by Tagore with a few lines of benediction in his handwriting, a letter Jawaharlal Nehru once wrote to my father, a few paintings by Nandalal Bose, Gauri di, Jamuna di and Vinayak Masoji, and two splendid water colours gifted to me by Abanindranath Tagore and Nandalal Bose when I got married—all these I have distributed to my children.

Yet, there are a few precious things that I cannot bear to part with. Among them are two long letters from Manik da written on handmade paper in his beautiful writing. A few months ago, after a fan sweet-talked me into lending them to his wife, who was researching Ray's work, I foolishly handed them to him. 'I will return them in two days,' he had promised and then never came back. I waited a few more days, then—with the help of a friend in the police—I managed to retrieve them. They are both safely back in my hands now, along with a photograph of the two of us when Manik da came to Lucknow to shoot *Shatranj Ke Khilari*.

Years ago, when he was a little boy, Manik da had taken his autograph book to Rabindranath Tagore. Tagore wrote these lines for him:

Bahu din hare
Bahu krosh doore
Bahu vyaya kari
Bahu desh ghume
Dekhite giyachchi parvat mala
Dekhit gayachchi Sindhu
Dekha hoy ni chakshu moliya
Ghar hote shudhu du pa pheliya

Ek ti dhaner shisher bindu
Ek ti shishir bindu

[I walked for miles
for many days,
spent time and money to see
mountains, seas and oceans.
I saw everything there was to see
but never saw the drop of dew
swinging from an ear of paddy
in my own field]

How prescient Tagore was when he wrote those lines! Satyajit Ray went all over the world, criss-crossed the earth to see the most magnificent mountains and oceans. And yet, he never forgot the beauty of that dew drop on his rice field at home.

Seemanter Sindur

It's often said that behind every successful man is a woman, but if that woman is also his wife and fellow traveller, you can take it from me that his success will be assured in every way.

Acharya Hajari Prasad Dwivedi's brilliance and scholarship were so well disguised by his humility and simplicity that he brings to my mind those anonymous Kumartoli sculptors who fashion the statues of the eight-armed Durga at the pujas that bring thousands to marvel at the life they manage to breathe into each idol they create. Yet, no one knows their individual names.

Bhabhi ji had a name—Bhagwati Dwivedi—and she was just thirteen or fourteen when she entered Pandit ji's life. Ever since, she faithfully followed him like a shadow, protecting his tall and imposing body from any harm. I am reminded of a stanza her husband once taught us in class:

Avgun ek mor main mana
Bichurat pran na keen payana
Nath so nayananhi ko apradha
Nisarat pran karhi hati badha . . .

How would she stay alive after him, I used to wonder, for in the last few years, when Pandit ji was a broken man both physically and mentally, she had become even more vigilant about his health. She would not leave his side even for a day.

'When I must eat, what I must eat, when go to bed—your Bhabhi has made strict rules for me to follow,' he grumbled once when he visited me. Sitting on a takhat with his legs folded under him, he said, 'The older she gets, the more she is turning into a police *ka daroga.*'

'If I don't police him,' she retorted in her lovely sing-song Bihari Hindi, 'do you know what he'll do? He'll eat rice at both meals, put a fistful of sugar in his tea, slyly get some sweets and accept every invitation to speak at literary gatherings anywhere. He'll go off to Calcutta, or Bhopal, and even as far as Hyderabad when his doctors have warned him against travelling so much. Tell me, what can I do but become a daroga in his life?'

Something frightened me as I listened to her stout defence that day. What if she were to die before him? Who would take care of my beloved guru then? I knew from personal experience that there is no way one can ensure that the person who is your protector is not taken away before you. I was just recovering from my husband's untimely death, and I silently prayed that Pandit ji would not be cheated by death the way I had been. Please, God, I prayed, let her remain his daroga forever.

I had been noticing disturbing signs in him for the last few months: he'd begun to pant and wheeze as he climbed the stairs to my flat. Often, he would suddenly lapse into a moody silence in the middle of a conversation. The Hindi

Sansthan had created a web of worries for him to deal with. These related to those humdrum bureaucratic details that his simple, honest and trusting nature was not equipped to handle. So, like Shiva, he swallowed all the nasty poison spewed by the audit teams to save the organization from shame.

All this made Bhabhi ji furious. Once, when they had both come over for dinner and I was frying puris in the kitchen, she called out, 'Ai Gaw-raa [she always called me that], come here for a bit.'

I took the puris off the fire and went in to find Pandit ji looking very grave, pretending to read a magazine, and Bhabhi ji's fair, round face puce with anger. Just minutes ago, I had left them happily seated next to each other on my takhat. What had happened since?

'Look, he's not slept all of last night—Sansthan, Sansthan, Sansthan! The wretched place has ruined his peace of mind. Give it up, I told him, throw away this bag of troubles, leave! He signs wherever anyone asks him to and all the problems land at his door. Now why don't you speak?' she turned on him. 'Isn't this the truth?'

What could I say? My silence infuriated her. 'He won't sleep all night and wakes up with a raging headache. If I say something, he says he'll take a headache pill or something for his blood pressure. As if that is going to give him peace! I know that until he gives up that wretched Sansthan work, he won't get any peace or relief.'

'My puris need my attention,' I made a weak excuse to bring down the temperature in the room. 'I'll just get dinner on the table.'

Throughout the meal, I kept her attention on the food and didn't let her go on another tirade against the Hindi Sansthan. I could see that she watched every mouthful he took like a hawk. 'Did you take any potatoes? Is that extra salt I see you've hidden under the puris?' she asked him.

Then she turned her attention to the generous helping of kheer that I was spooning out for him. 'Hain, hain, what are you doing?' she admonished me. 'Don't give him a full *katora* of it! Bas, just one spoonful for him to taste, that's enough.'

Poor Pandit ji looked at me helplessly as he watched his daroga put back all the extra spoonfuls into the serving dish. 'Just let me eat it today,' he begged her. 'One day's extra helping won't do any harm. Gaura makes delicious kheer,' he cajoled her, 'just try some yourself.'

'Oh ho, now I know why he can't stop talking of your cooking when he returns from Lucknow. You feed him this kheer every day when he comes here, no?'

Pandit ji sent me a frantic look, as if to say, 'Don't tell her the truth, please!'

'No, Bhabhi ji,' I lied. 'Don't I know he's not allowed to eat sweets?'

'Hmm, I must say you've blossomed into a good cook,' she said. 'Remember the time when you set a karahi on fire cooking spinach in my kitchen? You left in terror with the flames smoking the place.' Long ago, in Shantiniketan, I was hovering in her kitchen when the dhobi arrived. 'Here,' she told me, 'just put some hing, methi and mirchi when the oil starts smoking and put in the spinach. I'll go and take care of the dhobi's account.' I did as she had told me but was totally unprepared for the fire that leapt from the wet leaves when I put them in the karahi and ran away.

Of course I remembered those days; I even remember the first time I met her. She must have been just twenty-five or so with a round, fair face that often turned red. A dainty nose with a plain gold pin, tightly plaited hair that came down to her waist, and a simple sari tied with the pallu in front. A paan in her mouth stained her lips red and a huge red bindi and vermilion adorned her forehead. They had just three children at the time and I still call them by the names they had then—Babua, Putul and Titil. The other half of their simple cottage belonged to Gosain ji, whose young son Viru had tragically died there. The courtyard on Pandit ji's side had a drumstick tree, and in the summers, Bhabhi ji used to cook under the shade of that tree on a small makeshift *chulha*. This mobile kitchen soon became an adda for all of us students from Uttar Pradesh.

I have no idea how she managed to feed us perennially hungry hordes. As soon as she saw me leading this locust-like lot, she'd mutter, 'Here she comes again, this maharani leader! Come sit here so I can feed your baraat.' Yet how lovingly she served us! Dollops of ghee were put into a dal that seemed to us like ambrosia from heaven. In *sawan*, the rainy season, she'd grind a huge ball of henna to put on our palms and swing along with us on a swing we rigged from the trees in front of the cottage. Every Wednesday, when the Ashram was closed, I'd arrive at her doorstep.

'I knew it,' she'd tell Pandit ji. 'She's like a shameless stray dog that can smell food from a mile off. She knows I make karhi every Wednesday.' After this strange greeting, she'd pile a huge mound of rice and pour a generous helping of her delicious karhi on my brass thali. 'Even if you hadn't come,' she told me, 'I'd have come over with your share to your hostel.'

She loved both of us sisters, but my elder sister, Jayanti, had a more elevated status in her eyes—for instance, she was never asked to run chores like me; I had to do all the odd jobs for Bhabhi ji. She'd toss a fresh puffed-up roti at my thali straight from her chulha and I had to be ready to receive her bouncers so that they did not land on the floor.

'Ai Gaw-ra,' she'd give me a list, 'just run along to the cooperative and fetch me these things. You can keep one anna, and take Babua along with you, get him some lozenges for two paise.'

I hated these commands.

'No, I won't go,' I muttered. 'You've drenched Babua's hair with so much oil that it is running down his face and on top of that he's wearing such a long kurta that you can't see his knickers. People will think he's naked underneath that kurta.'

But there was more. Babua wolfed down his sweets with the speed of light and then insisted I buy him more from the commission that was mine. If I didn't give in, the wretched boy would throw a tantrum right there in the store, rolling on the floor as he bawled to attract attention.

'Oh, I see!' his mother said. 'You've become such a memsahib now that if Babua's kurta is a little longer than your highness can tolerate, your reputation gets sullied. Go!' she told me. 'Run away to your hostel and don't you dare come here again begging for a meal.'

I gave in and took the hateful brat to the store.

Almost every other day, the Ashram had a rehearsal for some dance drama that was being prepared—*Chitrangada*, *Chandalika*, *Mayar Khela* or *Valmiki Pratibha*. Bhabhi ji loved watching these rehearsals, and whenever she came, I was given the responsibility of keeping a place from where she and the children could watch the play. If there wasn't enough place for all of them, she'd send Putul and Babua to sit with me. 'Go, sit with Bua and watch the play,' she'd tell them. I can recall Putul's sweet little face because she invariably dozed off sitting on my lap. I'd hand over the sleeping child to Bhabhi ji at the end of the performance and get a firing. 'Got her to sleep, na? I knew you'd do this!'

'I didn't do anything,' I said. 'She dropped off on her own . . .'

'Dropped off on her own indeed! Couldn't you have nudged her awake? Now tell me, how am I supposed to lug this sleeping child back to the house?'

I never met Putul after I left the Ashram, but a few years ago, Babua came to my flat. I could hardly recall the brat he was when I knew him last. 'You've become an old man, Babua,' I told him. And when he laughed, I heard his father's famous guffaw after an age.

And Titil? She had made me cry once. That year in our intermediate exam, the question paper was especially tough. I went to Pandit ji that evening, 'Not only did you not teach us how to answer those questions, even the others were horrible,' I complained. 'I won't get a first division, I know, but I hope I pass at least.'

'Don't be silly,' he pooh-poohed. 'This is what you say after every exam.'

But I went on whining until he got fed up. Finally, to get rid of me, he suggested: 'All right, then, let's ask Titil. She's never wrong.'

Titil was duly summoned and asked, 'Tell us, Titil, will Bua pass or fail?'

Titil rolled her large, solemn eyes and declared without hesitation, 'She will fail.'

I burst into tears. Pandit ji didn't know what to do to stop my tears. 'Don't be silly,' he said, patting my back awkwardly. 'Has anything Titil said ever been true? In fact, she predicts the exact opposite of what happens. Listen,' he called out urgently to his wife, 'just look at this girl's drama and see her *dhuluk-dhuluk* tears.'

Bhabhi ji came and gave me an earful as a scared Titil watched. 'How stupid is this, hain? How can you believe a four-year-old? Go, wash your face and run back to your hostel. Now!'

At Durga Puja, when most of the students went home, the Ashram turned into a virtual graveyard. However, Gurupalli, where our teachers lived, buzzed with joyous activities. The smell of new, starched saris, the aroma of home-made sweets from every house, along with the cool breeze of the season, lifted our spirits. Bhabhi ji bought new clothes for her entire family and took me as her private secretary on her shopping sprees for, right to the end, she always trusted my taste in clothes. She'd send word that she was going to Bolpur the next day and I was to be ready. That tiny market was, for us Ashramites, like the famed souks of Baghdad.

We lived so far away from Bengal that we were unable to go home for the Puja break, so this was a welcome distraction.

I loved going to Bolpur with her. Sarojranjan Chaudhry was Pandit ji's neighbour and the owner of a gleaming black car. It had been decided that he would drop us off at Bolpur on his way elsewhere and pick us up later. In those days, car owners were rare, and he treated his precious car like a treasure. No one was allowed to even touch its shining body, and he himself, dressed in a starched kurta with gold buttons and a pleated, gold-bordered dhoti, would personally drive it. He drenched himself in so much perfume that the whole car reeked of it. He patted the steering wheel and asked us yokels at the back, 'So? What do you think of my apsara?'

One of the great treats offered by Bhabhi ji was the prospect of a 'dubbul amlate' she'd get me at Bolpur's little eatery grandly named 'The Grand Hotel'. What had inspired the owner to christen it 'Grand' was a mystery—everything there was so tawdry that it was pathetic. Its walls were made of bamboo mats, and along with an ancient rickety wooden table and two-three benches was a board that had its name scrawled on it along with the menu in Bengali that could be translated as: 'We sell a double egg omelette here'.

Its chef-cum-owner-cum-waiter was as old and doddery as the furniture. He had all of three teeth in his mouth, a lovely smile, a balding pate, two bow-shaped arms—in short, he was as grand as his hotel. The minute you entered his shack, his arms that looked as if he was gripping a steering wheel whirred into action—khat-khata-khat.

'So what will you have, Didimoni?' he asked, as if he was expecting you to order a five-course meal.

'Amlate?' and khat-khat-khat went his hands as he beat the eggs. 'Hen or duck?'

We knew that his duck egg omelette was huge and so fluffy that it seemed as if it was filled with air, so we settled for that. He'd break two eggs into a bowl and then beat them so rapidly that his fingers became a whirr, like the blades of a fan. Then he chopped onions, green chillies and coriander with the same speed and added a tablespoon of milk to the mixture. A battered frying pan went on the fire next, and into it he lavishly added ghee from an old cigarette tin. Then started the most fascinating part of the preparation—he poured the egg mixture into the pan, swirling it around to cook it and then, without a spoon or a spatula, he tossed the omelette into the air so that it flipped and landed neatly in the pan again. To me, he was like a magician who takes a coin and says, 'Here it is and now it's gone!'

We held our breath until the flying omelette landed safely in the pan.

'There, Didimoni,' the magician smiled toothily as he placed it in front of me, 'eat it up for you'll never get an omelette like this anywhere else in the world.'

However, that day, Bhabhi ji constantly intruded into this idyll. 'Hurry up, girl,' she hustled me. 'We have still to buy the saris, and Saroj Babu will arrive on the dot of three.' I quickly swallowed the last delicious mouthful and we got up.

The next stop was my classmate Viswanath's shop, so how could I not stop there? He used to hand me a bagful of sweets for one anna if his father wasn't around. That day, fortunately, he was the master of his shop. Bhabhi ji pursed her lips, 'Wait, you rascal, just let your father return and see if I don't tell him how you loot his shop to please pretty girls.'

In those days, Bolpur had just one sari shop and the owner spread out the entire collection for us to choose from. I found a lovely green one with a broad orange border and dainty stripes. The price? A mere 7 or 8 rupees! Suddenly, the canny owner took out another bundle and said to Bhabhi ji, 'Choose one from here, Ma, these are the latest designs that I've just opened for you.' Bhabhi ji looked uncertain and ready to be seduced by his sweet cajoling. A bright yellow sari with a wide red border that had lotus flowers and creepers woven into it caught her eye. The red was the same colour as the vermilion she wore on her forehead and she couldn't resist it. But it was expensive—15 rupees.

Her face fell when he told her the price because she had just 10 rupees left in her bag. She picked it up, weighed the price and her dilemma and then said, 'Leave it, I don't have the money for it just now.'

'Go on, take it, Ma,' he persuaded her. 'You can always send me the money later.'

'No Bhabhi ji,' I told her firmly. 'Please don't waste your money on this rustic sari. Please.'

'Quiet,' she told me. 'Rustic sari indeed! I love the red flowers. Do you know this red is called *seemanter* sindur—the symbol of eternal *suhaag*!' She threw away my green sari and picked up that hideous yellow one instead.

On Ashtami, when she wore the sari, even I had to admit she glowed in that colour. Her mouth was stuffed with paan, a huge red vermilion bindi adorned her broad, fair forehead, her wrists jingled with red glass bangles while her head had the same vermilion filled into the parting.

After this, she never failed to point out how often her friends and neighbours had borrowed that sari to wear. Her neighbour, one Alo di, came wearing it one day. Bhabhi ji nudged me and said, 'See? And you called it a rustic choice. This is the third person who's borrowed it from me to wear!'

Some forty years later, I had the pleasure of accompanying her on another sari expedition. They were staying at a flat in the Raj Bhavan complex after Pandit ji had returned from Calcutta. I went to meet them there and opened her tin trunk to see what saris he'd bought for her.

'This girl will never grow up,' she laughed. 'She has to poke her nose into my clothes.'

All that the modest trunk had were three wrinkled cotton saris, thrown carelessly between a shawl and a tin of Pan Bahar.

'Shame on you, Pandit ji!' I said. 'You were given such a grand award, the Rabindra Samman, and your wife still has the same saris she had years ago.

'I'm taking these home,' I told her. 'I'll get them starched and ironed and bring them back tomorrow.'

'Put them right back,' I was told. 'I've ironed my silk sari for tomorrow.'

I said nothing as I walked over to her bed and lifted the mattress. This is how she always ironed her saris.

'I am not so stupid that I should waste money on dhobis and ironing,' she sniffed when I looked at her.

'Wah! Just look at the ironing you've done.' I showed her the wrinkled folds. I heard a loud guffaw from Pandit ji.

'Go, buy her a nice chikan sari. She's always wanted one. How much will it cost?'

'At least 150,' I said.

'Why do you listen to her?' she scolded her husband. 'A cotton sari for 150! What utter rubbish! I'm sure I can buy one for 30–40 rupees.'

'Then go and buy it yourself,' I told her. 'Are we talking of a chikan sari or a Banarasi *gamcha*?'

'Ai, Gawra,' she warned me. 'Don't teach me about saris. Give me 50,' she told her husband. 'I'll buy one that I can afford.'

After another heated argument, we settled for 100. 'It's scorching outside,' I told Pandit ji. 'We'll die if we go in this weather in a rickshaw to Aminabad. Your official car is outside. Can't we go in that?'

'No!' he thundered. 'That is an official car meant for me, not for buying saris in Aminabad. If I'm not in that car, you two can't sit in it.'

'Then come along with us,' I wheedled. 'People will think you've come on some Sansthan work.'

'So that you two can buy rewri-gajak as well, hain? No arguments now, go!' he shooed us off.

'Why do you waste your time arguing with him?' Bhabhi ji said in a long-suffering voice. 'The others in the organization happily let their wives go all over in the official car but not our Raja Harishchandra.'

Once, long ago, when he came to my house in a rickshaw I wrote in my weekly column that it was a shame that a scholar of his eminence had to move around in a rickshaw because the Hindi Sansthan that wasted thousands on non-activities could not provide a car for its most famous member.

'Why did you write that?' he scolded me. 'So what if I had to take a rickshaw?'

'I'm so glad you wrote that,' Bhabhi ji patted my back. 'If Indira ji had been around, would they have dared to do this?'

She was right. Pandit ji himself used to tell me how Indira Gandhi always gave her full attention and respect to the gurus of the Ashram. Not many after her have had the grace to honour the national treasures we have among us, especially our scholars and academics.

So we took a rickshaw and I felt I was back in Bolpur on another sari expedition with Bhabhi ji. I took her to Netram's shop for jalebis and then to a paan shop near the Shiv Mandir from where, I told her, paans were sent regularly for Kamalapati Tripathi ji.

She rolled the famed paan in her mouth and endorsed my choice. 'This is really good, a real maghai paan!'

We landed up at Chhangamal's chikan shop and he pulled out a mountain of exquisite saris for us to choose from. Sadly, they were way beyond Bhabhi ji's modest budget. Her face fell, exactly as it had in Bolpur all those years ago. He got another lot and I picked up a beautiful pastel almond-coloured one. What is more, it was within our budget too.

'This is such a pale colour, old women wear such colours,' she whispered to me. 'Choose something brighter.'

'I thought this colour was exactly right for someone of your age,' I teased her.

'I'm not buying for myself,' she confessed. 'I'll give it to my daughter-in-law. She's been longing for one and she is young, of an age to enjoy nice saris. But don't you dare tell your Pandit ji.'

I don't know whether her daughter-in-law liked the sari we chose that day, but I'll never forget how generously her mother-in-law gave away the one chikan sari she would ever be able to buy.

A few months later, Bhabhi ji arrived at my flat but was in a big hurry. 'Here, this is for you,' she said as she handed me a bag of goodies. 'This is the roasted chiwra that you love. We are going to see a girl for our younger son today.'

'Can I also come along?'

Pandit ji said generously, 'Come, come. But don't take long to get ready.'

'No, don't take her along,' Bhabhi ji said. 'This memsahib will find a hundred faults and if she doesn't like something, she'll say it right there.'

'Have you forgotten how you used to drag me along on every shopping trip to Bolpur once upon a time?' I reminded her.

'I will still take you along to buy saris but not to select a daughter-in-law,' she told me sternly. Then she burst into laughter and said, 'What are you staring at? Hurry up and get ready. We're getting late.'

'No, not today, Bhabhi ji,' I excused myself. 'I have to go somewhere,' I lied.

I had never intended to go but Bhabhi ji was right. Accompanied by two such wonderful people, I was sure I would never find someone to match up to their stature.

Some months later, when I went to Hyderabad, I met Titil who told me her mother was ill. She'd become very anaemic, I was told, and they found out only when she passed out one day. When Pandit ji brought her to Lucknow for a check-up, he came alone to meet me.

'Come with me,' he begged, 'and knock some sense into her head. I've managed an appointment with the doctor but she says she won't go. She won't even agree to a blood transfusion.'

Pandit ji's face had turned dark with worry, and for the first time I saw signs of ageing in his bent back and defeated posture. I had never seen him so downbeat.

'Pandit ji,' I ventured to ask. 'It's not . . .?'

'No, no,' he cut me off before I could pronounce the dreaded 'C' word, 'it's not cancer. She has pernicious anaemia, she's had to take several transfusions.'

I went to see her to find her calmly making paan for herself—she was exactly the same as before. Then our eyes met and she transmitted that she knew she had heard the knock of death on her door.

'No more pinpricks,' she declared firmly. 'I've decided that. As it is they've punctured my arms like the lemons I make into pickle. Look!' And she bared her arms with dark blue blotches where needles had been poked in.

'Do I look ill to you?' she asked.

With great difficulty we managed to take her to Medical College. That was my last meeting with her.

I had no idea that she, who was all packed and ready to go, would be preceded by the one person she never wanted to be parted from.

I received news of her death from my friend, Thakur Prasad Singh, who wrote:

I've just returned from Banaras. Pandit ji had left us, but a few months later he was followed by his wife. When I went to the house one evening, I stood outside it for it was locked. There was not a glimmer of light to be seen in that huge place. About a year and a half ago, Pandit ji had said something to me that moved me immeasurably as I gazed upon that dark, lonely house. He said he hated leaving Banaras because he loved that house and was afraid that after he went, there would be no one to light even a lamp there. Every time he stepped out of the house, he would turn around to fold his hands to the Devi in his puja room he called 'Chatpati Devi', because he believed that she always ensured that whatever he had stepped out for would be accomplished immediately. *Chatpat se*, immediately, he used to say. I am sure he asked her to take them one after another, chatpat, so that they could be united chatpat . . .

Perhaps this is what did happen, I thought.

I am sitting today in my dark house and my conscience is rebuking me. How many times had I resolved to visit Bhabhi ji and him but never gone? There were so many times after he passed away when I thought of going to her and falling into her loving embrace. Was it so necessary for me to go to Indore instead, and for what? An award? How could I have not run instead to console my Gurumata, my Guru's wife, who loved me like a daughter? Then my head takes over and says how could you have let down the people who were giving you that award? Those organizers who had invited an audience and spent so much time and money on printing the invitation cards, booking a hall and arranging your travel? I had fallen ill after my return from Indore and by then it was too late.

Today, I feel perhaps it was just as well I didn't go to Banaras to meet Bhabhi ji. Her forehead without her red

bindi, her hair parting bereft of vermilion, her wrists bare
of red bangles—all my life I would have been haunted by
what widowhood had done to her. I turn instead the pages of
my memory album and see her as she will always be for me:
her mouth stained red with paan, her wrists merrily jangling
with glass bangles, her bright red bindi matching her Bolpur
sari with the red border and lotus flowers and creepers.
And woven into that mishmash of colour is a line that says:
'Seemanter sindur, *akshay hobe*' [Your sindur will be eternal]'.

The Bell Tolls for You

Just before his death, Tagore had said, 'I consider it a heresy to believe that death ends a man's life. The human spirit is beyond all this . . .' This profound truth has sustained me throughout my life and whenever I have lost a dearly beloved companion. Or, if I feel crushed occasionally by the criticism, slander and gossip about me and my work, I go back to his lines to revive my faith in myself. After all, I am not the only one in this wide universe who has had to deal with grief or failure. However, when I hear this from someone close to me, I must confess it takes me years to recover my poise. Remember the immortal lines attributed to Ravana as he spoke to his brother Vibhishana:

Janami sheelam jatinam sarvlokeshu rakshas
Drishyanti vyavseneshvete gyatanam gyatayaha sadam

[Know this, O rakshas! I understand the nature of all my brethren in this universe.
That it is your own kin that celebrate most when you stumble]

It is equally true, however, that if you keep dwelling on these pinpricks you will never be able to trust anyone. And I have known friends who have only brought me joy and solace and unfailingly rallied round me when I needed help. How often they have helped me up after a bad fall—these are the memories I want to cherish and keep as I grow older and wiser.

It is my misfortune that I have lost three Ashramites in just a year: Sushila Mehta, Arundhati Devi and Girdharilal.

Girdhari was with me in the Ashram from my earliest years right through to college. I had known him from my childhood as his father, Dr Hiralal Kothari, was the doctor to the ruler of Jasdan in Saurashtra. My father also served in the same court because its ruling prince, Thakur Bapa Saheb Alakhachar, was once his student in Rajkot's Rajkumar College. Jasdan was a small princely state, yet it had all the trappings of a proper royal court.

I was very young then but I have a fairly clear memory of those days. I can still recall the splendid interiors of the palace, the tall, strapping Arab servants in their unique garments sipping steaming cups of fragrant Arabian coffee. There were also scores of maids who always hovered around the glamorous royal consorts: the senior queen, Kamla Ba, and the junior queen, Madhavi Ba (a princess from Kapurthala) with her Bamberg georgette saris sparkling with sequins and gorgeous Baroda zari borders. Kamla Ba's only child was Lila Ba, who was about my age, and when Kamla Ba detained me once for two days in the palace to play with her daughter, I remember crying at night for my mother. Girdhari was also witness to those fairytale days. This is how, when we met in the

Ashram as students, we became friends once again. He was my class fellow and was fluent in Bengali because he had lived in the Ashram since he first started school.

In the Ashram, he was called 'Ghanta Kumar' because he was in charge of the Ashram bell. He knew all the chimes by heart, whether it was the deep sounds from Sinha Sadan or the gentle tinkles that summoned us to meals. The Ashram bell had a special grammar and code that he had memorized perfectly. He knew exactly when to sound the one for our morning prayer assemblies or the one for an emergency (ten loud and urgent ones) or the one we longed for, which marked the end of the school day.

He proudly held on to this post and over time, I think the deep notes descended into his throat so that he developed a very special speaking voice as well. Our morning prayers started with Jagatbandhu Krishnan leading the opening lines:

Esho hi jyotirmaya
Tomari hoke jai

His deep voice brought to mind the rumble of thunderclouds before a storm. After the morning assembly, Girdhari would run to sound the bell for the start of classes. As I have said before, each sound from the Ashram gong had a unique code which we were familiar with. This is why, when one day the 'emergency gong' was sounded, we all sat up in alarm. A few weeks ago, it had been sounded when Shyam mali, one of the Ashram's gardeners, was bitten by a poisonous snake. So all of us, teachers and students alike, ran out to see what had happened.

'What happened, Girdhari?'

Covered in sweat, Girdhari was still pulling the rope and he panted, 'A fire has broken out in the nearby Santhal village! Go, run, run!'

The village he referred to was just a short distance away from our Ashram, and since most of the houses in Shantiniketan had thatched roofs, it would have been disastrous if the fire spread further. All the students helped as buckets of water were organized and people ran helter-skelter to warn each other. I watched the sweating Girdhari and offered to help. 'Shall I pull the rope if you are tired?' I asked solicitously.

'Why aren't you helping the others?' he turned to me in anger. 'Don't you know this is my duty and mine alone?' and he twisted my ear to make his point. I had recently bought huge silver hoops from a Santhal mela and, despite the pain from an infected earlobe, wore them out of sheer vanity. After Girdhari pulled that ear, it started to bleed and he left his onerous duty to plead with folded hands, 'Please don't tell anyone I did this. I swear I didn't do it purposely. But you do know that I don't like to share this gong with anyone, don't you?'

I can still see his repentant face after all these years. I never said a word to anyone and carried the hurt for many years as a secret between us.

Recently, after a full forty-eight years, I went to the Ashram to participate in its Hindi Bhavan's Golden Jubilee celebrations and was appalled at the change that had swept over it. I somehow hid my deep disappointment, and as I opened one door after another, several beloved faces peered at me like ghosts from the past: Viswanath, Gaur Kishore,

Neelima Sen and Girdhari. And there he was, standing in front of me after almost half a century! 'Do you remember how I begged you once to not say a word to anyone after I pulled your ear?' he grinned as he greeted me.

'How can I forget?' I replied. 'You didn't just pull my ear, you almost tore it out of my head!'

'I remember it all,' he sighed in sympathy. He adjusted the thick glasses he now wore and explained, 'My eyesight never came back fully after a cataract operation. Imagine meeting you after all these years and not being able to see you clearly! Yesterday, Rajiv ji [Rajiv Gandhi] had come home,' he went on, 'and I couldn't see him clearly either. Now only Pupe and I stay here. We have a son, but he lives in Calcutta with his wife and our grandson. You know, Gaura, as you grow older and near the end, you sometimes feel suffocated by your memories.'

Pupe! He was referring to Gurudev's granddaughter, Nandini, my old and dear friend! She of the lovely face, whose plait swung to her waist, with large eyes and an incredibly innocent air. I was witness to their adolescent romance, and what a story that was!

Whenever Gurudev came to Almora, our home town, he stayed at what was locally known as the 'kankar wali kothi', near a most atmospheric little church. Far below in the valley was the leper asylum and the setting sun would flit over it, making its sad windows gleam with beauty. Tall, magnificent deodars surrounded the kothi, and a balmy breeze always seemed to blow around it. I spent almost the whole day with Nandini, who was my special friend, sitting on the cool steps of the church as we did our homework or sang songs. Pupe's

Nepali ayah would bring us our lunch and a flask of ghol (sour buttermilk that Gurudev always had for lunch) from the house as a picnic meal. Often, when we returned late, we were reprimanded by Bouthan (Nandini's mother and Gurudev's daughter-in-law, Pratima).

It was while sitting on those steps one day that Nandini confided that she was going to tell her mother she would marry Girdhari or no one else. 'I will remain unmarried for the rest of my life if they don't agree,' she told me solemnly.

I was stunned by her revelation for she was just sixteen years old then. She then handed me a thick envelope to post secretly. 'If Didi or Ma see it, I'll be in serious trouble, so be very, very careful when you post it.'

Those days, Gurudev's daughter Meera di and his granddaughter, Nandita Kriplani, had also accompanied Gurudev along with a friend of Nandita's called Jyotsana. I weighed the consequences of betraying the trust of so many people, especially Bouthan who loved me as much as she did her own daughter. I remembered how she had bought identical Jaipuri Bandhini saris for both of us last Puja and had said, 'Keep an eye on this one, all right? Make sure she pays attention to her studies. She's still very immature.'

I handed that envelope back to Pupe. 'No, I can't do this,' I told her firmly.

For the next two days, Pupe didn't talk to me and sulked. I also didn't go to visit her. On the third day, she arrived at our gate along with her ayah to fetch me. There was such a beguiling innocence in her that it was difficult to remain angry with her for too long. Naturally, I went.

Once we returned to the Ashram, she never mentioned Girdhari to me again but I could sense a change in her. She was no longer the immature spoilt child and appeared very aware of her changing body and feelings. A few months later, the Ashram was involved in preparations for another dance drama, and one of the songs set to a dance sequence was:

Esho nipavane chhaya vithi tale
Esho koro snan
Navdhara jale

[Come to the little stream in the forest
to bathe
in its sparkling waters]

Once again, Girdhari started hovering around Uttarayan, Tagore's abode. Then, suddenly, we heard that Pupe was engaged to be married. Her fiancé, Ajit Khatau, had seen her dance and fallen in love with her.

He was the son of a well-known textile magnate of Bombay and a handsome young man himself. Madame Sophia Wadia, a close associate of the Ashram, had proposed the match. All of Pupe's friends, including me, were involved in the preparations for her wedding. I was a little surprised that Pupe herself was most enthusiastic about her impending wedding. A letter that Gurudev wrote to Maitreyi Devi at that time says: 'The main topic here nowadays is Pupe's wedding. She is thrilled and while other brides-to-be often become bashful at this time our Pupe is not ashamed to show everyone how excited she is about her engagement.'

So what was all that letter-writing in Almora all about, I wondered. She showed me a beautiful gold necklace that Gurudev had given her, with an inscription in his own hand inside the locket. 'See?' she said. 'Isn't this just fabulous?'

I felt like asking her about those secret letters she used to post and her confidential chats with me as we sat on the cold stone steps of the church in Almora, but I just couldn't find it in me to spoil her mood.

Later, when I read Maitreyi Devi's memoir, *Swarger Kachakachi*, I learnt that there were some problems between father and son over the match.

She writes:

Gurudev had wanted a simple, no-frills wedding, yet although he had abdicated his feudal past, the son was still considered a Tagore, one of Bengal's most exalted feudal families. Rabindranath was staying with me in Mongpu those days when suddenly, Rathi da (Tagore's son, Rathindranath Tagore) arrived, accompanied by Shibu and Shambhu, an Airedale dog and a huge basket of betel leaves (because he couldn't survive without them and Mongpu didn't have any). Rabindranath was bent over a short story he was writing at his desk. The evening shadows were gathering and he didn't respond to the guests' arrival. Finally, he told me, 'I can't get up until I have completed this because I have a deadline to meet. I must send this for the Winter issue of Anandabazar and can't leave just now. They have promised me 100 rupees for it.'

Rathindranath did a lot for his father, more than what his daughters were able to. What his son and daughter-in-law, Pratima, meant to the patriarch is well known but he could not make his son do what he wanted for this wedding. The wedding was a magnificent affair, much against Gurudev's wishes. However, neither he nor his son were able to freely exchange or reconcile their views. Rabindranath would speak to us (me and his secretary of those days, Sudhakant Babu) but not a word to his son. Similarly, Rathindranath could never muster up the courage to speak openly to his father. He'd remove his shoes before entering his father's room and listen to him with his head bowed respectfully.

Rathindranath was aware that the huge expense of a traditional wedding was beyond his father's means and against his principles. So he came to me, 'Convince him, Maitreyi,' he begged, 'make him understand that he should just hand over the 25,000 he had kept aside for Pupe. It will be more than enough to meet the wedding expenses. I promise I won't dip into the Ashram's share.' But as far as I could guess, it wasn't merely a matter of money. Tagore was deeply pained at this meaningless show of pomp and splendour. I remember when he came after visiting Gandhiji's Ashram, he told me how they were offered packing cases to sit on. Such simplicity! And now, he talks of a traditional feudal celebration!

I tried to reason with him, 'Look, this is Rathi da's first and only celebration, it is unlikely that there will be another wedding in this family for a long time. The heavens won't fall if he spends money on it.'

'So, will you now join the ranks of those who counsel me to be worldly wise? Whether such a wedding is celebrated here in my Ashram or in Jorasanko is

immaterial . . . can you all not see how it will overturn my
life's beliefs and teachings? Can none of you understand
this simple fact?'

Anyway, a grand wedding did take place, and a huge pandal
was erected on the grounds adjoining Uttarayan. A screening
of *Gora*, Gurudev's famous novel, was held for us Ashramites
on the occasion and a lavish feast was spread out for the
groom's family and friends, served in shining silver vessels.
Every Bengali delicacy, made by the most renowned cooks
from all over Bengal, was offered to the guests, but Gurudev
sulked in his little cottage, 'Udichi', while all these frenzied
preparations were being made.

Maitreyi Devi gives us a glimpse of the tensions that floated.

Gurudev was hurt that I had come to attend the wedding,
so three days before the wedding I collected the sari that
Pratima had kept to gift me, and quietly slipped away.
Rani Mahalanobis (a close friend of Gurudev) also left
for Madras before the wedding. Pratima di kept asking
me, 'Maitreyi, did Baba Moshai say anything to you?'

What could I tell her? He'd said: 'I am appalled
that all of you are attending an occasion that deeply
saddens me.'

I caught his hint and left but later, when I saw
the wedding photographs, I was left completely
baffled. Sitting happily in the wedding mandap was
Rabindranath, with no trace of sadness on his face! But
I do know that he was never able to completely accept
this wealthy family into his austere life.

Girdhari went numb after the wedding but when Pupe came on her first visit after getting married, she was glowing. She chattered non-stop about the glamour and glitz of her life in Bombay. However, within a year, the marriage appeared on the brink of a break-up.

Many years after I had left the Ashram, I learnt that Pupe and Girdhari were married and they both had made the Ashram their home.

After having met Girdhari, I couldn't wait to see Pupe and be reunited with my dear childhood friend. Sadly, there was no trace of any memory in Pupe's face when I entered her room. I embraced her but it felt as if I held a lifeless doll in my arms. This could not possibly be the Pupe who used to drag me from home to spend the day with her in Almora, who chattered non-stop and giggled along with me over our girlish exchanges. She smiled blankly at me now. Girdhari quietly pressed my hand and said in Gujarati, 'Let it be. She's not in a nice place mentally.'

I was speechless with shock. I withdrew my hand from her limp clasp and realized that I had lost my Pupe.

'Perhaps I may never meet you again,' Girdhari said sadly as we parted. 'I don't have long now, my throat is always sore.'

'When did a sore throat lead to death, Girdhari?' I teased him weakly. 'You always had a sensitive throat. Remember how you would always wind a muffler around it in the old days? We have a lot to look forward to: you've just become a grandfather, who knows you may see your great grandchildren one day!'

'This isn't a case of tonsillitis, Gaura,' he told me seriously. 'I have a constant thorn pricking my throat.'

He wasn't wrong. Shortly after I met him, his son sent me news of his death: 'Baba is no more.'

I still have the Gujarati lines he wrote in my autograph book, years ago:

Biti maitreyi na smaran
Haiye rahi gaya

[All I have left are the memories
of our past friendship]

The writer of those lines has gone. But he was right: his memory remains.

A Song for a Friend

Another star fell off the skies—Arundhati. We spent a mere three years together but forged such a close friendship that it lasted our entire lives.

When I recall those days, it seems to me that the Ashram was immersed in music. I've seen all the great dance dramas Tagore wrote and directed from the time they were rehearsed to their eventual staging. Among them are classics such as *Chitrangada*, *Mayar Khela*, *Shyama* and *Tasher Desh*. There was no shortage of singers in the Ashram and Khuku di (Amita), Mohar (Kanika Devi), Smriti, Indulekha Ghosh, Vishni Jageshia, Suchitra—all of whom went on to become famous artistes later on—were my contemporaries. Added to their clear voices was the solid training of their native Bengali *jotdari*. Arundhati was tiny, fair and had huge dreamy hazel eyes that seemed to change colour from green to blue all the time. I still remember the first song she sang at the Ashram for us, a Baul composition:

Kanthe amaar, shesh ragineer, vedan baje, baul shejego . . .

The entire assembly was enchanted. She did not stay in the hostel but in a tiny cottage her widowed mother had rented at one end of the Ashram. She told us they were eighteen siblings and they were all over the place. Some of the sisters had been married off, some had gone abroad and settled down there. Just two of her brothers—Gopal and Badal—were students at the Ashram. Their lifestyle was entirely feudal: the way they dressed, ate and spoke betrayed their prosperous zamindari background. Their house was full of maids and their cook was an Oriya maharaj whose delicious food nourished us hostellers too. Nuku (this was her nickname) soon became a favourite companion, both for her generosity and her innate nobility. We used to call her mother 'Mashima' (Aunt) and I will always remember her as a very impressive woman. She spoke little but her large, sad eyes transmitted such love that we became as close to her as her daughter. She often sent us an invitation for a meal and watched over us, fanning us as we hungrily fell upon the food. She seemed to derive such satisfaction from feeding us that it encouraged us to become greedier and greedier. All of Nuku's siblings, barring the youngest, Probir, called 'Badal' at home, had the same glowing Anglo-Indian fair skin and hazel eyes. Whenever 'Vande Mataram' was to be sung at any celebration, Arundhati and I were called upon to lead the chorus. Our music teacher, Shailaj da, used to say, 'Your voices are a perfect match for each other. You must always sing such compositions together.'

Once, we were sent to Shiyuri village to sing. After a spine-jolting ride we reached the village, but by the time we were returning, it had got late and the sky had turned dark. Suddenly, a strong gust of wind blew out the hurricane lantern hanging from the top of the cart. There were others along with us in the bullock cart so it was not as if we were alone, but we'd heard it wasn't very safe to travel on these village roads after dark. We'd also been told that somewhere on the way there was a small temple dedicated to Attahas Devi, a deity worshipped by the dreaded Kapalik sadhus, who worship death and carry skulls to beg for alms.

Arundhati and I clung to each other in terror, although our coachman kept soothing our fears, 'Don't worry, Didimonis, I'll take you back safely to the Ashram.'

Another memory of her is when some of us Ashramites opened a tea stall at one of the melas that were held from time to time. All of us wore white saris and stuck a bright red hibiscus flower in our hair, which we wound into a low bun like Santhali women. Our menu was drawn and designed by Jaya Appasamy, who later became a renowned artist. A large crowd of customers lined up outside our stall, and poor Kalu, the Ashram's tea stall owner, came to us with folded hands, saying, 'No one is coming to my stall, Didimoni, all the Dada Babus are flocking here.'

We assured him that we'd wind up our stall by 4 p.m. and compensate him for his loss. An additional reason for the popularity of our stall was the snacks we were serving, many of them in those days a novelty for the Bengali palate: idli, vada, along with UP-style samosas and Bihari til-bhugga and anarsa. Sir Akbar Hydari came to our stall and we sold him a samosa for 10 rupees, a fortune in those days as the going rate then was about an anna for a samosa. Mrinal di (Mrinalini Sarabhai), Burhi di (Nandita Kriplani), Leela Aipen, Marie Wong—a Chinese student at the Ashram—and many others were all waiting impatiently for their turn. Nuku and I were assigned one of the tables laden with these delicacies. Suddenly, I spotted a beautiful woman walking towards us, accompanied by a comical dwarf-like man. I nudged Nuku and whispered, 'Look who's coming our way, the Beauty and the Beast!' She laughed along with me but offered no comment. They came and chatted for a long time after sampling several goodies and then said to Arundhati, 'Ai Nuku, get us our bill.'

I was taken aback by their calling her Nuku. Did this mean she knew them? I was still mulling over this when she pulled my hand and said, 'Know what my friend called the two of you, Chhot di? Beauty and the Beast!'

I wished I could disappear into the ground then and there. How was I to know that this was the youngest of Nuku's older sisters who had come down from Calcutta and that the man I'd rudely called the Beast was her brother-in-law? He grinned and pulled me next to him and said, 'You know, you're absolutely right about my beautiful wife. I applaud your taste.'

His generous gesture shamed me even more. I met them again several times after this unhappy introduction, and each time he'd guffaw at the memory of my silly joke. In fact, that year he sent a huge pot of rasagullas and a beautiful sari for Puja, especially for me. Along with these gifts was a note in Bengali: 'Dear friend of my sister-in-law. This sari will look very nice on you. With love from the Beauty and the Beast.'

I still blush when I recall that crass remark. A few years ago, I met Arundhati in Bombay where she had come for a coronary check-up along with her famous husband, Tapan Sinha, the renowned film director. I went to visit her at Jaslok

Hospital and she told me how her beloved brother-in-law had passed away and that Chhot di now stayed in the Ashram. Arundhati was told she did not need a bypass so we celebrated the good news and caught up with each other's lives over a long, leisurely afternoon. She had starred in many Bengali films, won plaudits for her singing and directed several films, among them *Yatrik*, *Kshudista Pashan*, *Mahaprasthaner Pathey*, *Chhuti* and *Gopal*.

'One day I'll make a film based on one of your novels,' she promised me that day. 'You send me a synopsis in Bengali and I'll work on it.' That promise as well as a similar one made by Manik da (Satyajit Ray) were doomed to be broken. My novels still await their films.

That day, when I met her in Bombay, I was shocked to see that she had lost her glorious glowing skin and that those magical hazel eyes that used to fascinate us in the Ashram were now ringed by dark circles. She was a sad mockery of her lovely self now. The Shankaracharya said it all when he wrote:

Ma kuru dhanjan, yauvan garvam
Hariti nimeshe kalah sarvam

[Never boast of your wealth, friends or youth
All these fade with Time]

A minor stroke had left her with a cruel limp. She pointed towards them, saying, 'Have you noticed the state of my feet?'

I remember when Gauri di (the artist Nandalal Bose's daughter-in-law), who did the make-up for our dance dramas, had looked at Arundhati and declared, 'Ah! A true Mughal beauty!'

The only part of her beauty that remained unchanged were her lovely hazel eyes, which still sparkled with mischief. They reminded me of some untouched ornamental frieze that startles a viewer as it lies in an ancient ruin. She went abroad for treatment, I heard, then to Bangalore, where she was finally operated upon for blocked arteries. Sadly, she never came out of that surgery. So one day, without saying goodbye, my friend went far away. Very far away.

A Light that Doesn't Go Out

I had heard about Jaya being struck by cancer. Someone, I remember, told me, 'After she was diagnosed with cancer, she went to the Ashram. Now, I hear, she is in Delhi for treatment.' Although I was in Delhi when I learnt this, I was leaving early the next morning on a foreign trip and decided that I'd go and visit her after my return. But by the time I came back, she'd already left this world. I cursed myself for not having made the effort before I left but how was I to know that her end was so near?

My mind turned to our last meeting in Delhi a year ago at the beautiful home of another Ashramite friend, Anita Grewal. I hid the shock I felt as I looked at Jaya's ravaged face. Dark circles under her lustrous eyes compounded by the deep sadness she seemed to exude. Perhaps she had already decided that she had little time left and had begun withdrawing from her old friends.

Many years ago, she'd popped up from nowhere at my house in Allahabad. She had just returned from a trip to China and managed to trace me when she heard that I lived in Allahabad. 'Look what I've brought for you,' she said as she produced a bottle of champagne hidden inside the folds of her shawl. 'We must celebrate our reunion after all these years in style, don't you agree?'

'Champagne, and for me?' I replied. 'How did you imagine that I'd jump for joy when I see it?'

'I should have known you'd remain the *dehati* you always were,' she sniffed. 'Doesn't matter, I've got you something else as well.' And out came an exquisite fan delicately painted with water colours.

I may have always been a rustic yokel but Jaya was ever the fun-loving sophisticate, even in our Ashram days. She was then a student of Kala Bhavan, painfully thin but blessed with a typical south Indian grace. Unlike some of the glamorous beauties among us, she had a quality that transcended her plain looks, and in no time at all, she became a very popular part of our gang. She posed for Ramkinkar Baij, the famous artist and sculptor, and that statue is still part of the Ashram's art collection. She was equally impressive at our literary assemblies, and whether it was a friendly debate, a poetry competition or the Ashram picnics, she became the centre of them all.

I have mentioned elsewhere how once all of us, fed up of a daily diet of aloo-potol, decided to launch a protest. Since it was against the Ashram's code of conduct to raise slogans, we sought help from Jaya in devising a suitable attack. She quickly produced a series of fabulous cartoons and we all pitched in to put them up all over the Ashram. So, from the notice board outside the library to Sinha Sadan, the mess hall and the hostels, Jaya's delightful artwork caught everyone's attention. Among the characters were a weeping potato, girls drowning a monstrous potol in a lake, and a really funny one, with the potato saying, 'Save me, Gurudev! I promise I will never set foot in an Ashram thaali again!' There were also colourful posters with 'Fie potato!' and 'Fie potol!' written in beautifully ornamental Bengali calligraphy.

And then again, at a Paush mela, she had drawn up a terrific menu card to be pinned outside our tea stall. The most illustrious students of the Ashram lined up to savour the wares, drawn and described so evocatively by Jaya. It was a sell-out show! She was the one who had decided that all of us in the stall would wear white Bengali saris with red or orange borders and add a bright red hibiscus flower to our hair, tied up in the Santhali-style low bun. A jaunty Gandhi topi completed our 'uniform'. I still remember that menu:

Samosa: Chokher Bali
Halwa: Char Adhyay
Mihidana: Geetanjali
Chingri: Sonar Tori
Chai: Nauka Doobi

All the titles were taken from Gurudev's works and were hugely appreciated.

And what a voice she had! She could easily match the highest notes of the male voices and soared over them like a nightingale. I cannot forget her beautiful rendering of one of Tagore's famous songs:

Ogo aamar shraban megher
Kheya torir maanjhi

I used to get irritated with her pronunciation though and always corrected her when she said 'maji' instead of 'maanjhi'.

At Anita's home that day, I asked her to sing that song for us. 'And don't you dare say "maji" again,' I laughed.

'I don't sing any longer,' she said sadly. 'I've lost my voice and parts of my memory too. My knees give me such pain sometimes that I fear I may even forget to walk very soon,' she added with a touch of her old self.

How was I to know that cancer was slowly hollowing out her body and mind? She may have been born in south India but her real birth took place in the Ashram, and whether she was in the Lalit Kala Akademi or in China, she always returned to the Ashram, like a child seeking a mother's loving embrace when in pain.

A few years ago, I read an article in the Bengali magazine *Desh* where an art critic had traced the history of modern Indian art and divided it into three eras. The first stage (1900–30) was the age of self-discovery. Our own artistic tradition had been virtually erased by the onslaught of Western art. Like a comatose ruler who has lost touch with his own people, we had forgotten the glorious art traditions of our ancestors. It was due to the herculean efforts of nationalist painters like Abanindranath Tagore and Nandalal Bose that the embers buried in the ashes of the past were reignited. The second stage (1930–40) was the celebration of folk art, pioneered by Jamini Roy. The third (1940–49) belonged to Binode Behari Mukherjee, Ramkinkar Baij and Amrita Sher-Gil, who gave a new direction to old art forms and raised searching questions through their work. The years that followed were full of angst and a search for a modern idiom in which to depict the confusion and difficulties of a modern industrial society.

I knew Jaya well and realized that she was truly above personal ambition and self-promotion. She was secure in her world and knew where she stood in this pantheon. She lived and worked in a clean, uncluttered and austere world and never sought state recognition and awards.

I recall how once she and I had jointly won a prize from Gurudev at a poetry competition. 'Isn't it sad, Jaya,' I said to her at our last meeting, 'that both of us who were awarded for our poetic efforts by one of the world's greatest poets never wrote poetry again? You took to painting and I to writing novels and short stories.'

She laughed, 'Are you referring to those childish poems we wrote long ago?'

I have in my hands a beautiful painting she gifted me once long ago as a birthday present. It's a small work, and at its centre is a small lamp, glowing with a flame that lights up the encircling gloom of the ledge it is placed on. It seems to me now a lamp lit in memory of a loved one to remind us of the departed soul. How wrong I was when I told Jaya it was a pity that she never wrote poetry after that competition. What I hold in my hands is a poem in another medium.

A River that Lost Its Way in Sand

The hot summer has melted into an unbearably humid rainy season—whatever happened to the refreshing coolness of the month of Asadh, I wonder, mopping my brow. Then, out of the shimmering heat, a beloved face floats out and I can hear her voice reading Kalidasa's immortal lines from *Meghdoot* to me: '*Dhrumjyoti salilmar . . .*'

Jayanti was the second of us seven sisters. Early this year, news of her terminal illness reached me in Lucknow and I rushed to Delhi to her bedside. What I saw shocked me—gone was the glowing olive colour of her skin and her musical voice was now a whispered croak. She held out her thin arms to embrace me and started to weep. I had never ever seen her cry and we both realized that this was probably a prelude to a final separation. As I held her trembling body, I felt unable to bring myself to say anything. We both knew it was too late for that.

She drew back, passed a loving hand over my head and said sheepishly: 'I don't know what happens to me nowadays, the waterworks just don't stop. How are you?' One claw-like hand clasped mine and the other trailed like a withered creeper across the bed. Her arms had become so thin that the bangles slithered up to her shoulders. Her eyes, clouded with cataracts, were straining to focus on my face and I was almost glad that she could not see it. Nor could I answer her loving question. With a long sigh, she folded her arms over her chest, closed her eyes and withdrew to some inner world.

Earlier, whenever she did that, Jayanti would be meditating, and her face would turn luminous with peace. It was her secret way of communing with her inner self and her mind. And what a mind! Banaras Hindu University once conferred the degree of Sahitya Mahishini on her. From her childhood, she had lived with our grandfather, an eminent scholar of Sanskrit, and her skill at languages was legendary. Gujarati, Bengali, Marathi, Urdu, Hindi, English, Sanskrit, Pali, Prakrit—she was fluent in all. At Shantiniketan, she studied Chinese under Professor Ta'an but Sanskrit was her mother tongue. When she wrote, it was like a piece of jewellery: sparkling and pure. So, in her old age, when her hand started to tremble and her half-blind eyes no longer obeyed her, it made me weep to read her scrawl. Reading was her life and when her eyes failed her, she died a little each day.

For some reason, she never pursued her skill at storytelling. Had she done so, I am convinced she would have been one of the finest writers of her generation. *Chand* and *Hans* had published her early writing, and one of her stories was included in the academic syllabus of Viswa Bharati University, but then for some inexplicable reason, she stopped writing. Her collection of letters alone was fit for a museum. Premchand, Jainendra, Rabindranath Tagore, Nandalal Bose,

Alice Boner, Acharya Kripalani, Madan Mohan Malviya, Balraj Sahni—Jayanti used to correspond with all of them. How I wish I had asked her for these letters before she died. I cannot remember how many letters Acharya Hajari Prasad Dwivedi had written to her. Gurudev painted a portrait with colours she herself had collected from wild plants, after consulting the *Vanaushadhi Parva* of the *Amar Kosh*.

Last year, the Bengali magazine *Desh* published a letter by Tagore where he mentions how his beloved student Jayanti had collected haridra, khadir, palash and burunsh to extract vegetable colours for his paintings. I sent her a cutting. When I met her a few months later, I asked, 'Did you read that article?'

'I can't find it,' she replied. 'I'd put it under my pillow and it seems to have disappeared. What did it say?' she asked me disarmingly.

I shook my head in exasperation. Her 'pillow bank' was a notorious Bermuda Triangle where things mysteriously vanished. You could find everything from dried fruits to old photographs and forbidden sweets (she was diabetic). Surrounded with such distractions, what could that poor article have done but disappear?

Jayanti's tragedy was that she never gave her genius the honour it deserved. That honour was given to it by Gurudev and the gurus of our Ashram. Hajari Prasad Dwivedi used to say, 'One day, Jayanti will inherit my pen.' Gurudev had nicknamed her Bharat Mata, or Mother India. With her thick khaddar saris, hitched inches above her ankles, her abstracted gaze and remote expression, she evoked laughter from some and envy from others. Her closeness to Gurudev was for all to see—he showered her with such love and attention that many declared Jayanti had become proud.

This was not true—pride and Jayanti could never be synonymous. Although, God knows, she had every reason to be arrogant. She was beautiful, accomplished and respected in the Ashram. Her beauty—which shone through the hideous homespun saris she wore—was incandescent. This was evident from the proposals that my mother began to receive when Jayanti passed her intermediate exam. But Jayanti had announced long ago that she would never marry. My mother used to coax her, saying, 'Look, Jayanti, proposals such as these don't come every day—where will you find such boys and such families? You are eighteen; your elder sister was a mother at fourteen. This boy has gone abroad to take his ICS exam . . .' But Jayanti was adamant: she would never marry.

Among her suitors was a dandy, nicknamed 'Lord', who found many excuses those days to pass by our house. I remember how livid Jayanti was when she saw him—resplendent in a tweed jacket, cigar in hand—eyeing her from the road outside our house. 'Listen,' she told me. 'I'll give you 5 rupees—spit on his brilliantined hair and tell him, "My sister will never marry you."' I accepted the offer with alacrity—5 rupees was a lot of money in the '30s. The next evening, Lord came on his usual evening stroll and stopped outside our house—as he often did then—preparing to strike the appropriate posture for gazing at Jayanti. I had lovingly nursed a ball of spit in my mouth all evening for just this occasion. The missile went flying out of my mouth and landed neatly on his pomaded locks. 'Scram,' I yelled rudely. 'My sister has said she will never marry you.'

That was the last we ever saw of him but I still blush when I remember my uncouth behaviour. Years later, the poet Sumitranandan Pant wrote a story on Lord's proposal in a collection of stories called *Paanch Phool*.

Meanwhile, Jayanti was determined not to marry. She had passed her MA by now and was offered a wardenship at Shantiniketan, where she also taught. Most of her time, however, was spent with Gurudev at Uttarayan, and whenever he went to Mussoorie or Almora, Jayanti was his constant companion. When Mahatma Gandhi visited Shantiniketan, Jayanti was chosen to receive him. A photograph taken by the famous photographer Shambhu Saha shows Gandhiji getting out of his car, his hand on Jayanti's shoulder, Ba on one side and a loving Rabindranath looking on.

Last year, I asked her, 'Where is that picture? Or is that lost as well?'

'God knows who flicked it from my album,' she said ruefully.

'And that poem written for you by Gurudev from Darjeeling? Where is that?'

'Lost as well,' she said.

I used to get livid with her—what treasures she had managed to lose! Yet there was one she never let out of her sight—this was a portrait of her painted by Tagore with the colours she had mixed for him. Inscribed '*Jayanti ke, Rabindranath* [To Jayanti from Rabindranath]', it was always on her bedside table.

Come to think of it, Gurudev was not wrong when he named Jayanti Bharat Mata—she was a born social worker. I have lost count of how many students she taught and how many destitute girls she educated and married off. Her husband was a doctor (yes, she did marry later. It was a fairly radical event for those days) and they lived in an idyllic house in Mukteswar in the Kumaon hills. They had a garden full of flowers and fruit trees, dozens of helpers—Jaikishen, Bishandutt, Daulat, Salim—and two fat Australian hybrid cows. Virtually all of Mukteswar had free access to her dairy and there was no expectant mother who did not receive a pail of pure milk from there. She would make the most delicious rasagullas and sandesh and I can vouch that even Bhim Nag and Bambajari in Calcutta never produced anything like her sweets. Married to a doctor, Jayanti naturally offered free treatment and medicines to everyone.

I remember a particularly gruesome incident. A grass cutter was attacked by a bear which clawed out his nose while the man was out in the jungle. However, his doughty wife packed the mauled nose in snow, and husband and wife landed up at her house (I had come to spend a vacation with Jayanti those days) at two in the morning. It was bitterly cold and a snowstorm was raging outside. Several tall deodars, unable to bear the weight of the snow on their branches, had snapped like matchsticks and keeled over. Power lines had collapsed, and there was no light anywhere except for the deathly white glow of the snow around us. Only the truly mad would venture out on a night like that.

Naturally, we stepped out, and the half-frozen woman, holding up her fainting, noseless husband, fell at our feet. 'Help me, Dactrani-jyu,' she called out to Jayanti, 'please save my man's life.' I took one look at the hideous, noseless lump of bleeding flesh in front of us and ran inside. Within minutes, there was blood all over the verandah, squirting in a steady stream from the hole in the man's face. Jayanti came inside to persuade my sleeping brother-in-law to take the poor man to the hospital and he erupted furiously. 'Who can I call to the hospital at this hour? You know I am on leave. Tell them to go to Dr Sen.'

'How can you say this?' Jayanti was livid. 'I don't care if you are on leave or not; you have to take him there.' When she gave orders, everyone listened to Jayanti, I can tell you.

Her husband tried to wriggle out by saying, 'I'll take him in the morning. Tell them to go and sleep in Daulat's room.'

'I'll assist you.' Jayanti would not be dissuaded. 'And you know perfectly well that Daulat won't allow even a bird to share his room.'

She was absolutely right. Daulat was a part of my mother's huge retinue, now with Jayanti. For twenty-five years, he had spread terror in my mother's household. Finally, she could take no more of his filthy temper and packed him off to Jayanti's house. Daulat's effeminate ways were the talk of the town and when he draped his dhoti over his head and snaked his way down a road, people would openly titter at him. My older brother used to call him Damayanti but with a temper like his, perhaps Durvasa would be a more appropriate nickname! He ruled over Jayanti's kitchen like a tyrant and his waspish tongue could flay the skin off someone's face. When Jayanti lost her favourite pen, she sent someone to ask Daulat whether he had seen it. 'Yes,' was the reply sent through the trembling courier, 'tell her I am signing the chapatis with it!'

There was no question of Daulat allowing anyone access to his room at that hour of the night. So my brother-in-law,

Jayanti and I stumbled with the injured man and his wife to the hospital in the freezing cold at two-thirty in the morning.

'Where is the nose?' my brother-in-law asked.

'Here,' said the wife, and carefully unwrapped it from a fig leaf. It took about two or three hours to suture the nose back on to the man's face and I was amazed at my brother-in-law's courage in tackling the job, without proper assistance, no lights and just his wife and a hysterical twosome as audience. Would any modern surgeon even dare to take on such a job? Miraculously, the man recovered, and why not? How could there be any chance of an infection when nature itself had sanitized the whole atmosphere with a thick blanket of snow?

Two years later, the grateful patient returned, a huge grin under his restored nose. In his hand were two containers for the doctor and his wife—one with fragrant honey and the other brimming with pure ghee from his village.

Another time, the X-ray technician lost his wife at a game of cards. The poor girl, a pretty young thing, came sobbing to Jayanti. 'Save my honour, Dactrani-jyu,' she wailed. 'This bastard has sold me for 3000 rupees!' The perpetrator of this crime stood next to her, weeping and speechless with shame. Jayanti saved his wife but forbade her to go back to her husband. She arranged to have her trained as a nurse and gave her an income to live a life of honour and independence. Years later, I used the incident to write a story called 'Piti Hui Gote'.

Then came the doe-eyed Sujata—slim, sultry and siren-like. Married to an alcoholic much older than her who used to beat her every day, taunting her childlessness by saying, 'Whore, you haven't even produced a mouse in the four years we have been married,' Sujata ran away and arrived at Jayanti's doorstep. Dressed in the *ghagra-choli* of a village belle, she was quite an attractive bundle. My mother took one look at her and said sharply, 'Jayanti, pack her off right away, I tell you. Otherwise you will regret your generosity. I don't like the look of her—her *nara* is dangling and that, my child, is the sign of a harlot.'

But once Jayanti made up her mind, could anyone persuade her to change it? Within a year, Sujata became a different thing. Her large eyes were lined with kohl, her hair sported a saucy red flower and the ghagra was replaced by a sari with a jaunty pallu that fluttered with every step she took. I renamed her Sujata, after the famous Bimal Roy film of those days, because she reminded me of the actress Nutan.

My mother's prophecy proved true. Sujata first fluttered her eyes in the direction of my mother's house. My elder brother's cook, a handsome young man called Dilip, was her first victim. When the vegetables started to burn, Jayanti realized that she must cut short her visit to my mother's house before worse things happened. Sujata was taken away but her lover could not bear her betrayal and Dilip committed suicide. Eventually, Jayanti's husband and children told her that Sujata must leave. Jayanti agreed reluctantly but got her a job as a Gram Sevika before abandoning her to her own devices. She was followed by another siren, and finally, Jayanti vowed never to take on the cause of young women. Then, as if to test her promise, a madwoman landed up at her doorstep and refused to leave. She would lie around the verandah, singing, dancing and generally entertaining the house. Apparently, her husband's affair with another woman had turned her mind crazy. 'I stole all the jewellery and wear a loincloth, hahaha . . .' she told Jayanti one day and vanished. A few days later, they found her body on the streets. After her came a leper from Bhimtal—he was installed under an apple tree in the garden. 'I know Dr Moses of the Almora Leper Asylum,' I told Jayanti. 'Let me send him there, you must think of your children and husband too.'

'No.'

It was like this with her ever since she was in school. When we were in Gujarat, my mother had adopted an orphan girl called Panchi Bai. The village headman had left her in my mother's care after she lost her parents in a flood, so my mother became her 'Ba' (mother in Gujarati).

'Ba,' Panchi Bai declared one day. 'I want a man.'

The whole house was stunned at this shameless declaration. All except Jayanti, of course, who went and found her a suitable boy, another orphan called Jiwaram. One day, Jiwaram arrived, resplendent in a saffron turban, and stood with folded hands before my mother to seek Panchi Bai's hand.

Jiwaram had no home and no job. 'How will you look after her?' my mother asked this hopeless suitor. He looked bashfully at the ground and replied, '*Annadata*, you are there, aren't you?' So Panchi Bai was married—my mother gave her the dowry she would give a daughter and the *barat* started at our front door and went round the house to end at the kitchen door. Jiwaram was given driving lessons (Jayanti organized that, of course) and he became our driver.

When we went to Tikamgarh, Jayanti picked up a girl called Lalita, who had just one good eye. After her husband abandoned her for this reason, Jayanti took her in hand. She groomed her, taught her and within a year, Lalita was a changed girl. One day, her husband saw her at a fair, fell in love with her and took her back!

Meanwhile, in Rajkot, Jiwaram and Panchi Bai embarked on Project Family with such enthusiasm that within a few years there were several children—Popat, Radhabai and God knows who else. Then, tragedy struck and Jiwaram died of TB. Where else could poor Panchi Bai go but to her Ba's home? She arrived with her football team and stayed on for thirty years, travelling with us from Bangalore to Almora or wherever my father's work took us. Finally, she retired to her beloved Kutch.

After my father's sudden death, Jayanti became the head of the family. Our education, our travels across the country—all of this became her responsibility. Sometimes I wonder how she did it all. Yet I always knew that she was a born mother and that ultimately she would not be able to resist domestic bliss. Years ago, worried about her vow of celibacy, I had consulted a mendicant who used to visit us from time to time. 'Yes, your sister will marry one day,' she had said emphatically to me.

Jayanti married someone of her own choice but in her inimitable style, and after great opposition from the family. My brother-in-law was a handsome surgeon—Westernized in his education and bearing, he had had a brush with tuberculosis in his younger days. TB was considered a curse then, a sure sign of an early death, but Jayanti cared for no one's advice. She and her husband were devoted to each other and when she lost him a few years ago, she lost her own will to live.

After her husband's death, she only visited me once or twice, and when she came to Lucknow to receive an award from the Hindi Sansthan, all our time went in remembering the past. It was on the same trip that two of her Buddhist friends came visiting. The two monks had travelled from Gorakhpur to ask her to read two manuscripts in the Kharoshti script, which she did in minutes, translating them effortlessly into Sanskrit. On a trip to Kathmandu, she composed a Sanskrit hymn in praise of Pashupatinath and gave that to the priest as an offering. At the age of seventy-five, she trudged up 14,000 feet to visit the temple of Tunganath and recited some rare Sanskrit slokas to the priest who fell at her feet. 'Ma, you are Saraswati,' he said to her in awe.

'No, not Saraswati, Pujari-jyu,' she replied, 'just her devotee.' The more I remember what she was, the more I feel Jayanti was, in Tagore's words, a river that lost its way in the sand.

She was in unbearable pain in her last days. Her feet were swollen, for her kidneys had failed, and she would float in and out of consciousness to look around her restlessly when she was awake. I stayed a few days and then when I went to say goodbye to her before leaving for Lucknow, my eyes filled up. She could recognize me but her sad eyes were dry. I think the searing pain of one's last few days dries up all of one's tears. And that sad face, shrunken and forlorn, is the one that floats before my eyes when I recall her now.

With time, I feel, relationships have changed radically. I don't see in this generation the love we had for our siblings. We fought, said cruel things to each other but when it was time to part, we felt as if a limb had been cut off. My sister

Manjula and her husband had moved in with Jayanti to look after her, but she was away that day. So was Jayanti's devoted son, Pushpesh, who had to go to the university for a lecture. So she and I spent one last day together. She bared her heart for the first and last time that day. Her loneliness after her husband's death, and what it was like for her to be cut off from her children's lives and the world around her—all this and more . . .

'You had once written in some story that a man's umbilical cord is cut twice—once when he leaves his mother's womb and the second time when he gets married,' she smiled and pressed my hand gently. That touch said more than a thousand words to me.

Finally, it was time to leave her.

'Jayanti, I am going,' I said softly. She looked at me with unseeing eyes and turned her head away. She had withdrawn from this world already.

I am told she returned to her old self a few days before she died. But I am haunted by that last goodbye—her touch transferred all her pain to me that day. Lying alone in a house, no loved ones around her, all she did was live in the past. Shantiniketan, Shillong, Bangalore, Orchha, Rajkot . . . Do you remember, she asked me that day, Ija's sweet voice singing:

> *Aaj to sapna ma mane*
> *Dolna dungar divyajo . . .*

> [I dreamt of the
> rolling mountains today . . .]

With death hovering over her head, I am sure she could see the mountains we saw from our grandfather's courtyard in Almora—Kamet, Nanda Devi, Trisul, Banari Devi . . .

God knows what pain she suffered and took with her when she died. And perhaps it was this that took her mind into a peculiar direction. She began to take an unhealthy interest in other people's lives, a weakness cruelly exploited by some relatives. They would first encourage her to talk ill of someone, then it would be spiced up and spread around. So one heard often, 'Jayanti said this or that about you . . . she's become senile . . .' and so on. But how many, I wonder, saw her brilliance? Or her heart that was as clean as a mirror? So generous that she gave away all she had to whoever asked for it. Did anyone ever realize that she gave away so much that finally she had nothing left for herself? They stopped giving her money because she spent whatever she had in hand. She had already donated all her pension—yet she swore that a yogi had once given her a 'magic tortoise' that would always keep her in clover.

'Touch a copper penny to it and it will turn into silver,' he had told her. We used to titter behind her back but nevertheless went furtively to touch its metal back. I myself tried it many times, and I have to tell you it worked. Some forgotten royalty cheque or other would land up after that magic touch.

A few months before her death, knowing how she yearned for the old days, I told her, 'Jayanti, you have a cottage in Bhowali. Why don't you go back there? Isn't it better than lying alone here in Delhi? I may be younger than you but even

I know one does not die of any disease, it is the memories of the past that eventually kill you.'

She smiled through cracked lips, and that smile went like a dagger to my heart. She took my hand in her trembling and feverish clasp and whispered:

> *Sar sookhe, pachchi ure aure saran samae*
> *Deen meen bin pachch ke, kahu Rahim kahan jaye?*

> [Birds fly from a dry lake to seek another perch
> But where, O Rahim, shall a wingless fish flee?]